Insanity Once More

Insanity Once More

Lawrence Kudlow

Creators Publishing
Hermosa Beach, CA

Insanity Once More
Copyright © 2018 Creators Publishing

Cover art by Peter Kaminski

CREATORS PUBLISHING
737 3rd St
Hermosa Beach, CA 90254
310-337-7003

ISBN (print): 978-1-945630-87-3
ISBN (ebook): 978-1-945630-86-6

First Edition
Printed in the United States of America
1   3   5   7   9   10   8   6   4   2

A Note From the Publisher

Since 1987, Creators has syndicated many of your favorite columns to newspapers. In this digital age, we are bringing collections of those columns to your fingertips. This will allow you to read and reread your favorite columnists, with your own personal digital archive of their work. — Creators Publishing

Contents

Taxes Chased GE Out of Connecticut

January 16, 2016

But a big dose of free-market optimism can save the once great state.

GE's decision to leave Fairfield for Boston is another sad marker in the downhill slide brought about by Connecticut's high-tax, high-regulation, anti-business policies of the last 25 years.

Gov. Dannel Malloy accelerated the state's economic free-fall with another huge tax hike passed last summer. Despite his 2014 reelection promise of no new taxes, Malloy signed a $2 billion tax hike that falls heavily and businesses and individuals. This came only a few years after his near $1.5 billion tax hike.

Does anyone doubt that massive tax hikes on successful earners and corporations drive those same folks out of state? That's the new Connecticut story. A recent Pew poll shows that 60 percent of current residents want out.

Meanwhile, Connecticut's economy and rate of job creation have only recently recovered to pre-recession levels. So it took Connecticut eight years to get back even. Not new growth or new job creation — just even.

Hartford politicians don't understand that you can't have higher-paying jobs without successful businesses to create them. Punitive taxes on business, however, cause job shrinkage. Plus, you can't start a business without investment. Here, too, punitive taxation stops investment cold and ends the dream of more higher-paying jobs.

Who suffers from anti-business tax and regulatory policies? Middle-class families.

By the way, has anyone heard U.S. Sen. Richard Blumenthal, a career Democratic politician of 35 years, utter one peep of protest against Connecticut's ruinous decisions to punish business? Just asking.

But get this: From the Connecticut governor's office on down, Democratic officials argue that the GE move to Boston had nothing to do with taxes. Instead they say it was an effort to merge with Boston's high-tech culture.

There's a grain of truth to this, although Connecticut does boast Yale, Wesleyan, Trinity and Sacred Heart University's business school (named after great former GE CEO Jack Welch). But this taxes-don't-matter argument is malarkey.

When you tax something more you get less of it. Art Laffer's famous curve has kicked in with a vengeance in Connecticut, where higher tax rates are producing lower-than-expected tax revenues and killing jobs and growth.

It's no coincidence that well-to-do residents are moving to zero-income-tax Florida, and major corporations like GE are seeking greener pastures. It's also no surprise that GE CEO Jeff Immelt began talking publicly about a corporate relocation right after Connecticut passed its gigantic tax hike last summer.

That Democratic tax hike included a slew of corporate-income-tax increases, coming to roughly $500 million. At 9 percent, Connecticut's corporate tax is now fifth-highest in the country. And switching the state to combined-income reporting (including out-of-state GE income) was a killer. Additionally, sales taxes on everyone were raised while property tax credits were diminished.

Connecticut has the second-highest property tax in the nation, ranking 49th out of 50. The Tax Foundation ranks Connecticut 42nd out of 50 in terms of tax climate (Massachusetts ranks 24th), and second highest in terms of state and local income-tax collections per person.

Massachusetts? It dropped its corporate tax to 8 percent from 9.5 percent and has a flat income tax of 5.15 percent. Connecticut, on the other hand, jacked its corporate tax to 9 percent from 7.5 percent and its top income-tax rate to 6.99 percent from 5 percent.

These are sizeable differences in favor of Massachusetts. Taxes don't matter?

And the dirty little secret is that the pension and health-care benefits of the government unions — which dominate Democratic state politics — are roughly 50 percent unfunded. This spells many future tax hikes. GE's Immelt knows it.

Not all the blame goes to Democrats. Connecticut's first personal income tax was put in place by Republican Gov. Lowell Weicker. And Republican governors ruled for 16 years prior to Malloy's victory in 2010.

And in last summer's budget battle, I don't recall any Republican initiatives to slash business taxes.

One of the key points in the Connecticut disaster is that while big corporations can get $100 million in tax credits, the woman running a small struggling business in Naugatuck gets nothing. But she's paying for GE's tax credit.

Connecticut's high-tax policies do not soak the rich. The rich leave. Meanwhile, exorbitant tax and regulatory burdens slam the middle-class wage earners who have been losing take-home pay for years.

But you know what? This can be fixed. There are positive policy options. Connecticut needs a large dose of free-market capitalism. Roll back the overtaxing, overregulating, and overspending. It can be done.

But the political class in Hartford has to be overturned. Non-political citizens should run for office, vowing to restore incentive rewards for successful entrepreneurs, hard-working middle-class folk, and existing large and small companies. That will unleash growth, investment and risk-taking.

Change can return Connecticut to greatness. In fact, change can restore the national economy, too.

Let's get working.

We Will Never Destroy ISIS Without a Full-Blown Declaration of War

January 23, 2016

Speaker Paul Ryan's statesmanship may just get the job done.

The speed of the news cycle and the media obsession with the presidential horseraces have crowded out a crucial development in the war on ISIS and related Islamic jihadist groups.

House Speaker Paul Ryan has been appealing to colleagues for a new Authorization for Use of Military Force (AUMF). The current AUMF, which was written in 2001 and targeted groups connected to 9/11, has not been renewed. Believe it or not.

Bravo for Paul Ryan's statesmanship. But a new AUMF must be accompanied by a clear U.S. declaration of war against ISIS. We will never destroy them without a full-blown war declaration.

Now, there are important details regarding the AUMF. Ryan is correctly opposed to the Obama White House ISIS strategy, which would bar widespread use of U.S. combat troops in Syria and Iraq and would place limits on the length of military options. Sound familiar? It's Iraq and Afghanistan all over again. The new speaker won't stand for it. Good for him.

The White House wants to forbid "boots on the ground" and wishes to prohibit "enduring offensive ground combat operations." The use of special forces would be allowed, but that would expire after three years. In other words, Team Obama would tie the hands of the U.S. military and send all the wrong signals to our enemies.

But if the Republicans in the House and Senate show some backbone, they can get an AUMF without all the Obama prohibitions. Heaven forbid the Joint Chiefs be able to run a war.

This brings me back to the key point. In his pursuit of a new AUMF, Speaker Ryan *must* seek a formal U.S. declaration of war against ISIS. It is extraordinary that this has yet to be done. It should have happened 15 months ago, or surely after the horrific terrorist events in Paris.

I cannot understand why the president has yet to call an emergency NATO meeting to declare war on the Islamic State — which, by the way, has declared war on *us*.

But our president wants no part of that. Remember the Obama re-election-campaign narrative? Terrorism has been defeated and is no longer a problem. So how can you declare war on something that is not a problem?

Michael Flynn, recent head of the Defense Intelligence Agency and a retired four-star general, said, "I don't think enough people in our country see ISIS for what it is, and I think part of that is because our leadership has really denied the fact of who this is that we are facing. ... I think they failed to tell the truth."

The fact is this is the greatest national security problem of our time. Attacks from Europe to California have tragically proved that again and again.

So, how can it be that the Washington leadership has *not* produced a war declaration, which would surely rally the American people? A war declaration adds urgency, energy and immediacy to the war.

What's more, a war declaration would be a forcing device, outlining the American strategy with respect to the Islamic State and terrorism in general. What is it we want? How will we know when we get it? How does the war end? How long do we stay? What are our postwar intentions?

These are a few of the questions that must be asked and answered so that the American people will know what the American government intends to do. In this way, a war resolution will not only underscore the importance of this conflict, it also will help rally Americans to the cause.

It's a question of leadership, really. It's a question of commander-in-chief.

It's a question of congressional responsibility.

And it's a question for the presidential candidates in both parties. Answer it, please.

The White House and Congress must be truthful with the American people. No more pulling punches. A war will be a war, with the availability of all of our resources on land and in the air, and with the unfortunate reality of collateral damage in Syria, Iraq, and elsewhere. The great American military understands that costs must be suffered if American freedom is to be protected.

As retired four-star general and former Army vice chief Jack Keane recently told Congress, "There is no substitute for an effective ground force supported by air power. Air power is an enabler, not a defeat mechanism."

So we must do whatever it takes to destroy ISIS. Right now, it's not clear that the U.S. is winning.

This is both national security *and* homeland security. But we will not win this war unless we take the battle — in full force and without limits — to ISIS in Iraq and Syria. The best way to protect the homeland is to utterly destroy our enemies where they live.

The Fed Freaks Out About the Markets — Because It's Misreading the Situation

January 30, 2016

Early in the new year, on Sunday, Jan. 3, Federal Reserve Vice Chairman Stanley Fischer delivered a hawkish speech to the American Economic Association. Completely misreading the economy, which is woefully weak while inflation is virtually nil, Fischer strongly hinted that the Fed would be raising its target rate by a quarter of a percent every quarter for the next three years.

The next day Standard & Poor's 500 index dropped 1.5 percent. In the week that followed, the broad index fell 6 percent. The week after that it fell over 2 percent. During that two-week period, the Dow Jones dropped 1,437 points.

The dollar went up. Oil plunged 21 percent. Raw material commodities dropped. And credit risk spreads in the high-yield junk market rose substantially.

Actually, it was a global event, as stock markets around the world plunged. Utter chaos.

This past week, the Fed retreated in its Federal Open Market Committee policy statement. For the first time in a long while, it didn't bother with a risk assessment between inflation and employment. The whole statement had a much softer tone. It reminded me of the prevent defense of Bill Parcells' old New York Giants.

Putting it more starkly, I'd say the Fed is completely freaked out by financial markets that are turning against it.

The central bank says its policies are "data driven." But the recent FOMC statement suggests the Fed is looking at everything. It has a hundred indicators — domestic, international, jobs and inflation. In truth, it doesn't know what its next move is going to be, because it can't read the economy. Fed policy is opaque, confusing and rudderless.

Take a look at the new GDP report for the fourth quarter of last year: a mere 0.7 percent growth. Across 2015, real GDP grew 1.8 percent. It's not a recession. But any shock could push us into recession.

Business investment fell. Commercial building fell. Inventories fell. Inflation came in less than 1 percent.

Nominal GDP — real output plus inflation — registered a small 1.5 percent gain. In normal times, money GDP should be between 4 and 5 percent.

Perhaps most troublesome to the stock market and the economy is the decline in corporate profits. According to most estimates, profits are set to drop for the third straight quarter while business sales look to be falling for the fourth straight quarter. Add this to less than 1 percent economic growth, and the risk of recession is surely rising.

The recession threat is a risk, not a fact. But for Fed policy makers to tell us the economy is healthy is a complete misreading of the situation. And with ultra-weak economic growth and ultra-low inflation, how could the Fed, or any central bank, think about tightening policy?

Besides stocks, other market indicators are trying to tell the central bank: No more rate hikes. Copper is down 16 percent over the past year. Inflation expectations in the Treasury bond markets have fallen significantly. And the dollar over the past several years has increased roughly 30 percent.

A healthy King Dollar is a good thing, and so are falling energy prices. But enough is enough. More Fed rate hikes will raise the dollar and reduce energy prices so much that the economy will be completely disrupted. A stable, reliable greenback is a good thing. But let's not press our luck.

Now, if the Fed were operating on a true price rule, it would keep the dollar where it is today for as far as the eye can see. In turn that would stabilize gold and other commodities and avoid further economic disruption.

In a speech back in 2014, former Fed head Paul Volcker argued for a rules-based monetary policy along with international currency cooperation. Right now we have neither. Europe and Japan have moved toward negative interest rates while the Fed threatens higher rates. Where is Volcker's currency diplomacy? Nowhere to be seen.

Thankfully, there's a way out of this mess. Let the Fed keep interest rates and the dollar stable. No more tightening. Meanwhile, the Republican Congress can pass a significant tax cut for large and small businesses. Push the rate down to 15 percent for C-corps and S-corps. Provide easy repatriation of U.S. money overseas. And permit immediate tax write-offs for new-business-investment expenses.

Congress could also push for reduced regulatory burdens, although it looks like there's no stopping the Obama administration's unconstitutional march toward even greater regulations.

But a big business tax cut would be the most stimulative way to move the economy from near recession to 4 or 5 percent growth. That's what we need. Put it together with a stable and reliable dollar, and we can move from pessimism to optimism.

It's been done before. We can do it again.

Message Matters: Trump Succeeded, Yellen Failed

February 13, 2016

Most political reporters are fixated on the presidential horserace rather than the message candidates are sending to voters. Message wins all the time. Message moves polls. Message raises money. Message determines elections.

Most of all, a clear message tells voters what a candidate believes and where he or she wants to take the country.

Ronald Reagan was the master of the message. Campaigning on a few key points, he told America how he was going to rejuvenate the economy and defeat Soviet communism. He didn't spend much time on detail. But over and over he repeated his strategic message. It worked.

The two biggest events this past week were Donald Trump's landslide in New Hampshire and Janet Yellen's testimonies before Congress. Trump's message succeeded. Yellen's failed.

An unlikely pair, to be sure. But let's give a quick thought to *why* Trump got it and Yellen did not.

First up, Janet Yellen. Six weeks ago the Fed raised its target interest rate, with a lot of hawkish talk about three years of sequential rate hikes. Markets crashed in response. And now the Fed is in full retreat.

This is not a clear message. This is not leadership.

Before the House this week, Yellen acknowledged that the Fed's forecast and polices may not be working. (What an understatement.) She pointed to stock market declines and higher credit-risk interest rates. And when asked whether the Fed was changing its upbeat economic view that would lead to more rate hikes, she replied, "Maybe, but the jury is out."

Oil prices and inflation are falling. So are profits. No clear message.

The next day before the Senate, not only did Yellen back off additional Fed rate hikes, she raised the issue of pushing short-term interest rates into *negative* territory. Whoa. The flip-flop of flip-flops.

That policy hasn't worked in Europe or Japan, and it won't work here. It would destroy savers, again. Banks will go into short- and medium-term Treasuries, which at least have a positive yield, rather than make loans. And negative rates will crush net interest margins for banks.

The Dow fell 231 points following Yellen's stellar performance. Year to date, stocks are off 11 percent. And banks are off 18.5 percent. You're not going to breed economic confidence when the Fed leaves everyone in confusion.

Now let's leave Yellen in the emergency room and move on to a patient who has healed in the message department.

Donald Trump is today mastering the art of the positive. Coming out of an Iowa loss, campaign manager Corey Lewandowski told him bluntly, according to The Wall Street Journal, "We can knock on every door and call every resident. But most important: If we remain positive and focus on our message, we can win New Hampshire."

Win indeed.

When I interviewed Trump on the day before the primary, he emphasized his positive message of optimism, growth and national security. In recent weeks, he has talked about how America has been losing key battles around the world, whether it's ISIS, Russia, Iran, China trade, immigration or the declining economy. And he has loudly proclaimed: If you elect me, we will start winning again. Everywhere.

Asked what a President Trump would do about the risk of recession, he reeled off a series of tax cuts, deregulations and federal budget cuts. He knows the country is in revolt against Washington, D.C., and he plays to that with his program.

He talks about oil independence and opening up federal oil fields.

He talks about bombing ISIS oil trucks.

He mentions Anthony Scalia and Clarence Thomas as models for Supreme Court appointments.

He talks about creating jobs — over and over.

He talks about strong border controls to fix the illegal-immigration problem.

He talks about a strong military and renewed support for our military vets.

He proposes a total repeal of Obamacare, with health savings accounts and creating a more competitive market by letting citizens purchase health-care plans across state lines.

Perhaps most interesting, he is railing against big corporations and their big money deposited in super PACs. Unlike a typical Republican, he hangs out Big Oil, Big Pharma, Big Insurance and Big Lumber as examples of the corrupt monetary influence on American politics.

I asked him if he intended to change the Republican Party. He snapped, "You bet I do. It needs changing."

There are soft spots in Trump's proposals, most particularly on China trade. His tariff threat is worrying Wall Street and pro-growth free-traders such as myself. More work on that will come.

But apart from even these details, Trump's message is clear: America must start winning. And yes, we must make America great again.

Positive and optimistic. Growth. Leadership. Clarity. It worked in New Hampshire.

Janet Yellen, on the other hand, nearly fell off the financial ladder.

Message matters. There's a lesson here for all of us.

A Growth Message, Not Catfights, Will Propel the GOP to November Victory

February 20, 2016

In the week leading up to the New Hampshire primary, a few GOP candidates put forth strong, positive, optimistic messages of economic growth. Donald Trump did it, and it contributed to his landslide. John Kasich did it, and he surged to second place. Jeb Bush put his best growth foot forward, and he nearly took third place. Others, not so much, and their numbers sagged.

Growth is the No. 1 issue of this presidential campaign — even beating out national security, which is, of course, very important.

As Wall Street Journal columnist Bill McGurn recently put it, "A growing economy means a growing standard of living. ... That translates into more dreams fulfilled for more Americans, whether that means a college degree, a home in a decent neighborhood, or just the certainty that your children will do even better than you did."

In other words, strong economic growth leads to aspirational confidence for all people, but particularly the middle class, which is in revolt.

Charles Murray has written about a beleaguered working class, telling us that it is falling away. They are angry at the so-called "ruling class." They are getting a smaller bite of the economic pie, which itself is barely growing.

This is why the Republican candidates, who have barely mentioned growth in the run-up to the South Carolina primary, look so uninspired. They have stopped speaking to the worries, crankiness and anger of the middle class.

Whatever happened between New Hampshire and South Carolina, the GOP has lost its growth message. Instead, the race has become a huge catfight: Candidates snarling at each other. Charges of lying and dirty tricks. Fake images in campaign ads. Underhanded push-pull phone banks. Yelling at each other for something somebody said last year, or three years ago, or 20 years ago.

This is not aspirational. This is not leadership. This is not about growth.

A new poll from John McLaughlin, of national polling firm McLaughlin & Associates, reveals that the Republican rank and file don't even like their leaders. Donald Trump comes out ahead in McLaughlin's likability scale for the GOP. But even while leading, some polls show Trump is losing ground.

Columnist Fred Barnes frets that the Republican rift will not be healed and that the prospect of a GOP triumph this November is fading. He worries that Republicans are campaigning to lose.

But the central reason for this is that they've lost the optimistic and winning message of economic growth.

Economist John H. Cochrane of the Hoover Institution at Stanford writes in a recent essay that "sclerotic growth is the overriding economic issue of our time. From 1950 to 2000, the U.S. economy grew at an average rate of 3.5 percent per year. Since 2000, it has grown at half that rate, 1.7 percent."

Here's how important that is for the middle class: From 1952 to 2000, real income per person in the U.S. rose from $16,000 to $50,000. But as Cochrane notes, if the American economy grew by only 2 percent per year over that period, rather than 3.5 percent, real incomes for the average person would have risen to only $23,000, not $50,000. That's huge.

So with less than 2 percent growth in the last 15 years, real-income progress has been stopped.

The GOP should be quoting some of these numbers and hammering home the point. Reagan used statistics. But no one is using them now.

And it's not just the numbers. It's hope, optimism and leadership, too. The Republican message should be geared directly toward the discontent and pessimism that has taken over the middle class.

Just say it. And make this point clear: The problem is not inequality, as the Democrats would have us believe. The problem is the lack of growth.

This is not to say the GOP candidates don't have good policy ideas on reforming taxes, regulations and spending, and the need for stable money. They do. But they barely talk about these policies anymore. And when they do, they don't slam it home.

Even Democratic economists are attacking the high-spend policies of Bernie Sanders. He'll bankrupt the country, if we're not bankrupt already. And Hillary Clinton's program is not just Sanders Lite. Some economists have calculated that her spending plans would require a 69 percent personal tax rate. Average working folks know that will not grow the economy.

John Cochrane writes, "Solving almost all our problems hinges on reestablishing robust economic growth." The GOP must get back to this message — or they will blow the November election.

2 Percent Growth Is a Loser for the Angry Middle Class

February 27, 2016

The good news is that the economy is growing at 2 percent and that there's no recession in sight (barring a complete collapse of profits). The bad news is that the economy is growing at 2 percent. It's been doing so for nearly 15 years under Democratic and Republican administrations.

Coming off a deep recession, real GDP growth is averaging no better than 2 percent. After 25 quarters of so-called recovery under Obama, it has increased a total of only 14.3 percent.

Compare this to earlier periods. After the JFK tax cuts of the early 1960s, the economy grew in total by roughly 40 percent. After the Reagan tax cuts of the 1980s, the economy grew by a total of 34 percent.

And here's the killer: Real middle-class wages are still flat-lining. These folks get nothing out of 2 percent growth.

As I feared, subpar economic growth never really came up in the Republican debate in Houston, Texas. Rather than growth, we got more catfights. It's time to get serious.

In a recent essay, John H. Cochrane, a senior fellow at the Hoover Institution, wrote, "Sclerotic growth is the overriding economic issue of our time." He has numbers to back this up.

From 1950 to 2000, the U.S. economy grew at an average rate of 3.5 percent. That generated a massive gain in real GDP per person from $16,000 to over $50,000. A huge win for the middle class.

But as Cochrane noted, if the whole post-World War II period had grown at 2 percent, income per person would have increased from $16,000 to only $23,000 — about half of what actually happened at 3.5 percent growth.

There is a big difference between 2 and 3.5 percent growth. It's not abstract or theoretical. Essentially, the middle class has not gotten a raise in 15 years. In fact, a new report from Sentier Research finds that median household income of $56,700 (adjusted for inflation) at the end of 2015 is almost exactly where it was at the end of 2000.

Not surprisingly, the middle class is cranky and angry. And they are voting for change. Significant change. As in throw-the-bums-out change. That includes presidents, members of Congress, big-company crony capitalists, and corporate welfarists.

The middle class is saying the system is rigged against them, and they want to change who's running the system.

Much of this gets to the root of the inequality debate. Democrats such as Hillary Clinton and Bernie Sanders want to raise taxes on the rich, saying it will solve inequality. It won't. All that will do is significantly reduce incentives to work, save and invest.

But I say inequality is not the problem. The problem is a lack of growth. Middle-class people who haven't seen a raise in all these years don't want to punish success, and they're not jealous of those who have done well. They just want their piece of the pie.

And while the pie itself has stopped growing, the individual slices have gotten smaller.

Can you blame them for being angry and desiring radical political change? Nope.

Coming out of the caucuses and primaries so far, the economy has been the No. 1 issue. There's a message there. And the GOP has to address the issue of growth versus inequality. So far they haven't done it.

With the GDP report for the fourth quarter, which ended in December, we know that the inflation-adjusted economy has grown at 1.9 percent over the last year. Business fixed investment — the category that produces good-paying jobs — is growing at 1.6 percent. Low gasoline prices have helped consumer spending rise by

2.6 percent, but even that's not a wildly optimistic number. The inflation rate, meanwhile, is a measly 1.1 percent.

All this tells me nothing has really changed. But we can change this fast.

Research has shown that middle-income wage earners would benefit most from a large reduction in corporate tax rates. The corporate tax is not a rich man's tax. Corporations don't even pay it. They just pass the tax on in terms of lower wages and benefits, higher consumer prices, and less stockholder value.

So, as I've written a million times: Slash the corporate tax rate to 15 percent for large C-corps and small S-corps; go to immediate tax deductions for new investment; and make it easy for firms to repatriate their overseas earnings.

This would be the single-most stimulating program for reigniting economic growth. Principally, it's a middle-class tax cut. If you combine that with regulatory rollbacks and a stable dollar, within less than a year the U.S. economy can break out of its doldrums.

To all the GOP candidates: Please send this message. To my Democratic friends: Why not revive the legacy of the JFK tax cuts? It would be a whole lot better than punishing success.

A Response to Jonah Goldberg's Mistaken Claim of My 'Pauline Conversions' on Trump

March 11, 2016

My friend Jonah Goldberg has written a column entitled "Conservative Purists Are Capitulating with Support of Trump." In this piece, Jonah goes after me and Stephen Moore for allegedly giving up our free-market principles for what he calls "purely consequentialist reasons." I am not sure of the full meaning of this phrase, but it sounds like it means we've changed our beliefs because Donald Trump is the leading candidate in the GOP presidential race.

Jonah is an old and valued friend, and I respect and admire him enormously. In fact, I wish I could write as well as he does — even when he comes after me. But I want to set the record straight on a number of points where I think Jonah gets it wrong.

First, Steve Moore and I continue to oppose Donald Trump's trade policies. Even if his 45 percent tariff threat on China is simply a negotiating card, as Trump told me in recent interviews, we still think that's the wrong way to go.

Speaking for myself, I believe China is a major trade violator. The Chinese break all the rules. They counterfeit our goods, steal our international property rights and cyber-hack our industries and government. Something must be done about it.

But a 45 percent tariff would be a major tax on American consumers and businesses. It would probably do more damage to the U.S. economy than to China's.

Now, I think we need a very strong U.S. president to enforce current trading laws between the U.S., China and the World Trade Organization. And perhaps some targeted economic sanctions on Chinese companies could work. For example, the U.S. has decided to sanction Chinese telecom giant ZTE for trade violations with Iran. This is a more precise response to trade violations than a 45 percent tax.

Trump may well have the presidential leadership skills to solve the China problem without resorting to economy-wrecking tariffs. But at the moment Steve Moore and I disagree with him on this topic.

Second, Jonah argues that I have moved markedly in Trump's direction on immigration. Here are the facts: I wrote a piece in mid-December where I announced a much tougher position on immigration — a big change in my thinking. But this had nothing to do with Trump. It was all about the war against ISIS.

The full title: "I've Changed. This Is War. Seal the Borders. Stop the Visas." I argued for a wartime moratorium on new visas and new immigrants because of the substantial danger of ISIS terrorists infiltrating our system. The piece was written just after the horrific attacks in Paris and San Bernardino. I argued that until FBI Director James Comey gives a green light to new visas, and until we completely reform the vetting process for new foreign visitors, the borders should be sealed.

War brought me to this position. My only mention of Trump was when I disagreed with him for singling out Muslims. My proposal was based not on religion but on the threat of ISIS infiltration into the United States. There was nothing "consequentialist" about it.

Finally, I have for many months endorsed Trump's tax-cut plan. In particular, I like his business-tax-cut strategy, which includes a 15 percent rate for large C-corps and small S-corps along with easier repatriation and cash-expensing write-offs for new business investment. I think it's an excellent plan that would substantially grow the American economy and bring trillions of dollars in overseas capital back to the U.S., which in turn would foster millions of new jobs and faster growth.

What's more, a number of think tanks believe the biggest beneficiaries of a significant corporate tax cut would be lower-middle- and middle-income wage earners. They, by the way, have not had a raise since 2000, which is probably why they're opposed to trade deals and illegal immigrants, too.

In the Michigan Republican primary exit poll, 33 percent said trade expansion would create more U.S. jobs while 54 percent said it would take away U.S. jobs. But I prefer an economic-growth solution to this middle-class angst, not a protectionist program. And I think Trump's business-tax-cut package would lessen trade fears by providing wage earners with a significant pay boost.

Thus, yes, I have endorsed Trump's tax-cut plan.

On the other hand, I have not endorsed any GOP candidate. As a commentator on this race, I think it would be inappropriate to do so at this time.

So, in answer to my friend Jonah Goldberg, I believe I am sticking to my pro-growth, supply-side strategies of lower tax rates and free-trade. Regarding immigration, where I have changed my view, that's all about the war against ISIS.

I want to assure my friend Jonah that I have not experienced any "Pauline conversions on the road to a Trump presidency."

Slash Corporate Taxes First, Then Yellen Can Normalize

April 1, 2016

Speaking before a packed audience at the prestigious Economic Club of New York, Fed chair Janet Yellen basically announced that there would be no rate hikes for quite some time — maybe once before year end, maybe not. Her key point was that the global economy is worse today than it was in December, back when the Fed took its target rate up a quarter point. I think she's right.

I also think she is paying more attention to forward-looking, inflation-sensitive financial and commodity-market prices. This is good. Very good.

Yellen cited shrinking inflation spreads in the Treasury bond market, declining commodities (until recently), a flattening of the Treasury yield curve, and a stronger dollar. The sum total of these market-price indicators is stagnant growth and virtually no inflation. Hence, there's no need for the Fed to militantly raise its policy rates.

This price-rule approach is a lot better than the Fed's flawed models, which are based on a false tradeoff between lower unemployment and higher inflation. I've said it a million times: More people working does not cause inflation. Instead, more people prospering and producing makes the existing money supply less inflationary.

Austan Goolsbee, former chairman of the Council Economic Advisors, has long argued that Fed models have consistently overpredicted the economy. As a result, the Fed has consistently had to lower its forecasts in the face of stagnant 2 percent growth.

The possibility that Janet Yellen is escaping the defective Phillips-curve mentality gives one a bit of confidence, especially if she is watching market prices. She even noted in her speech that the Fed's favorite inflation indicator actually fell in February, and is up only 1 percent over the last year.

Now let me make a second point. Most financial-market people think the Fed's ultra-low target rates indicate ultra-easy money. They're wrong. The principal reason that market interest rates are so low is that the economy is stagnant and inflation is virtually nonexistent. Along with a strong greenback and falling commodity prices, you could argue that the Fed is tighter than anybody thinks.

I don't want more QE, which was a failed experiment. The fact is, rock-bottom interest rates generally indicate near-zero inflation and relative monetary tightness. If market interest rates were surging, that would be a sign of higher inflation, undoubtedly because the Fed was too easy.

Milton Friedman taught us this over 50 years ago. Interest rates are lousy monetary indicators. Better to watch the money supply or the velocity turnover rate of money, which can be captured by tracking nominal GDP. Over the past year, money GDP has increased only 3.1 percent. That's a sign of monetary tightness, not ease.

As free-market economist Alan Reynolds of the Cato Institute recently noted, government interest rates were rock bottom in the 1930s. That's because the Fed and most other central banks were way too tight.

Even worse today, having stuffed banks with excess reserves, central banks in Europe and Japan are punishing those banks with negative interest rates. They're also punishing savers. This is not good policy.

What we have now in these uncertain times is not so much a monetary problem as a major fiscal problem. In particular, corporate tax rates must be slashed in the U.S. for large and small businesses. We also need full cash tax expensing for new investment and an end to the double taxation of foreign profits.

This would rejuvenate economic growth. In the global race for capital, the U.S. would emerge victorious.

Incentives matter. I'm not just talking about 4 or 5 percent economic growth, but higher wages and stronger employment-participation rates. And my guess is that, as real economic growth jumpstarts, real interest rates would move higher. And that's when the Fed can follow market interest rates upward by raising its policy rates.

By the way, it's the same problem overseas. Europe and Japan and so many other countries are ignoring tax policies, which are in sore need of growth repair. Japan needs tax cuts across the board: corporate, personal, sales, you name it. Europe has relatively low business tax rates. But it needs to slash taxes on personal income, estates and retail sales. Negative interest rates won't do the trick, but new tax incentives to work, save and invest will.

o I support Janet Yellen's moratorium on rate hikes. But I wish she would be more outspoken about the need for corporate tax reform. If the U.S. economy starts moving back toward its potential — 4 or 5 percent economic growth over the next bunch of years — the Fed can normalize its interest-rate structure by following higher market interest rates which would respond to faster economic growth.

Not Just a War on Tax Inversions
but Also a War on the Middle Class

April 6, 2016

Does the U.S. government want to help American business? Does the administration want to help middle-income wage earners? Does team Obama want to grow the American economy at its historic 3.5 percent long-term trend? Apparently, President Obama's answer to all three questions is "no."

Those are the real issues behind the Treasury's latest militant attack on so-called tax inversions, where a U.S. company merges with a foreign firm in order to take advantage of the foreign firm's lower corporate tax rate. In this case, the attack is aimed at Pfizer, pending the $160 billion takeover of Allergan. Allergan is based in Ireland, which has a 12.5 percent corporate tax rate. Pfizer is based in New York. So the new combined entity will pay the Irish corporate rate, which is nearly three times less than the 35 percent U.S. federal corporate rate — obviously, a huge savings.

The answer here is simple: Slash the U.S. corporate tax rate and then the problem goes away. It's by far the highest of the major countries worldwide. We are not competitive. Canada's is 15 percent; China's is 25 percent, and Europe averages 25 percent. These companies owe it to their shareholders and their work forces to act in a financially responsible manner. But no, Team Obama wants to wage war against them.

So here's a question: Why does Obama want to punish business, rather than reward it? Why doesn't this administration want America to be the top global destination for investment? Why not have the

U.S. win the global race for capital instead of losing? President Obama always gives lip service to lowering the corporate tax rate, but he never specifies a particular rate or an overall plan. What's more, he is trying to force U.S. multinational cash abroad to pay taxes as high as 19 percent even if they don't bring the money home. And then, they'd still be taxes at 35 percent for the repatriation of their foreign profits. This is insane.

Many liberals argue that big U.S. companies don't really pay the top corporate rate. While this is sometimes true, it's mainly because, during recessions, companies lose money and get a tax loss carryforward that temporarily reduces their effective rate. But during economic expansions, when profits rise, companies then do pay the top rate. So, it's a bogus argument. General Electric, for example, may not have paid taxes for a couple of years following the Great Recession. But during the recovery, their effective rate was near 35 percent.

Then progressives argue that the corporate-tax cut is a rich person's tax cut. Utterly untrue. Numerous studies have shown that the biggest beneficiary of corporate tax cuts is the middle-income wage earner.

By the same token, companies don't just pay corporate taxes out of their own pockets. They pass them along in the form of lower wages and benefits to the work force, higher prices for consumers and lower stock valuations for investors. Again, the data show that wage earners get the biggest benefit, consumers second and shareholders third. One key reason why average wage earners have had virtually no pay increases in the past 15 years is the high corporate tax rate. That is why so many Americans are so angry with Washington: They want *big* change.

Corporate tax reform should include not just large C-corps but also smaller business S-corps and LLC pass-throughs. And nearly as important as cutting business tax rates is the need to simplify the inexplicably opaque and complex system. Big firms can afford tax accountants to avoid all the K-street cronyism and corporate welfare. Smaller firms cannot: They get the short end of the stick.

Corporate share prices should not be driven by political tax games. Profits, not Washington shenanigans, should be the mother's milk of stocks. And this shouldn't be a partisan political issue. Either we want to make America great again or not. Unfortunately, democratic candidates Hillary Clinton and Bernie Sanders oppose significant business tax relief. Much more promising: Leading GOP candidates Donald Trump, Ted Cruz, and John Kasich favor slashing corporate taxes.

Fortunately, nine months is all we have left before this tax nonsense comes to an end.

How Trump Turned Cruz Into the Establishment Candidate

April 22, 2016

Donald Trump's landslide victory in the New York GOP primary was a game-changer. It ended his Wisconsin slump and set the stage for an across-the-board sweep next Tuesday in Pennsylvania, Maryland, Delaware, Connecticut and Rhode Island.

Trump's vote count exceeded his pre-primary polling average by nearly 10 percentage points. Perhaps most important, the win gave him 89 more delegates for the RNC July convention.

So Trump is now the prohibitive favorite to win the GOP nomination — although there is still much dispute about this. But I believe, even if he comes up short of the 1,237 delegates for a majority, he will still get a first-ballot victory. There will be roughly 190 uncommitted delegates at the Cleveland convention. And Trump, with his art of the deal, can be very persuasive.

But what hasn't gotten enough attention following New York is how Trump did it and how it will enhance his position in the rest of the primaries. My theory is this: Trump cleverly turned the tables against Ted Cruz in regard to the nationwide delegate fight, especially in Colorado. Trump outflanked Cruz.

y calling the delegate-selection process "rigged," and arguing that Colorado had an election without voters, Trump turned a loss into a victory. Why? Because he put Cruz in the unenviable position of defending the status quo delegate-selection process.

Now, Cruz played by the rules in Colorado and elsewhere. And Trump was caught flat-footed, and to some extent was embarrassed by his own weak delegate-gathering team.

However, and this is the key point, Cruz argued time and again that the rules were the rules and that he simply played by them. And as Trump continually attacked the RNC rules as being undemocratic, disenfranchising to voters and products of an out-of-touch Republican Party, he put Cruz in the position of backing the establishment. A bad place for Cruz.

Moreover, in attacking the delegate process, Trump was able to restore and even enhance his position as the anti-establishment outsider. The agent of change — that's precisely what GOP voters favor.

Colorado was a bad delegate story to begin with. A planned direct primary vote was canceled. But a friend related to me the disturbing story of his moderate Republican brother, who owns a small railroad and who caucused for Trump. Trump won that local caucus by 60 percent. But as the process moved up to the county level then the congressional district level and finally the state level, Trump got *zero* delegates.

At a minimum, this process was wacky, convoluted and opaque. At its worst, it was rigged against GOP voters.

Other states have produced similar horror stories. And Pennsylvania may be positioned to deliver the most ridiculous. Whoever wins the direct Pennsylvania primary next Tuesday gets only 17 out of 71 delegates. So no matter who wins, more than 50 delegates will still be uncommitted. That's crazy.

Actually, I think the whole GOP selection process is crazy. Why not a simple, direct, winner-take-all primary election? The person with the most votes gets all the delegates. Nice and simple.

RNC chair Reince Priebus might want to think about this progressive democratic reform. After 100 years or so, it's time for a change.

But back to the Trump New York win. Trump trashed the current delegate system while Cruz defended it. It was bad politics for Cruz.

And Trump expanded his critique into a full-blown issues platform. In a Wall Street Journal op-ed, five days before the New York primary, Trump argued that the old order — the governing elite, the establishment and the special-interest donors, consultants, pollsters and pundits — are the same people who were "wrong on taxes, on the size of government, on trade, on immigration, on foreign policy."

In very clear terms, Trump connected Cruz with exactly those establishmentarian elites, which have bred so much anger and resentment in Republicans everywhere.

Trump completely outflanked Cruz while turning a *process* issue into a *policy* issue. The more Cruz defended the delegate process, the more Trump hammered away at his new theme: Cruz is defending the elite old order. In that Wall Street Journal op-ed, Trump charged that Cruz is actually a member of the very "Washington cartel" that Cruz criticizes.

And like other state primaries, the New York exit polls showed that 88 percent of voters were either dissatisfied or angry at government, while 64 percent wanted a president who was outside the political establishment.

Much of this may be unfair to Cruz's issue positions and beliefs. But the distinguished senator, in his defense of the status quo delegate process, made a serious strategic error. Heading into yet another Super Tuesday, Trump is making sure that error is compounded and magnified.

By turning delegate caucus defeats into an overall message victory, Trump has given himself a "yuge" leg up for the GOP nomination.

Growth Anemia: Blame a Collapse in Business Investment

By Lawrence Kudlow and Stephen Moore
April 30, 2016

GDP for the first quarter of 2016 came in at a paltry 0.5 percent. That sorry showing follows growth of 1.4 percent and 2 percent in the previous two quarters. If such a thing is possible, the already-anemic economy is actually getting worse.

But even worse than that, the latest GDP numbers reveal a collapse in business investment, the real driver of the economy.

When businesses don't spend and invest, they don't hire and cannot offer better-paying jobs. Business investment and wages are two sides of the same mirror. If a company purchases five trucks rather than 10, there are five fewer trucking jobs. If employers don't invest in more computers, there are fewer programming jobs. If businesses don't purchase more jackhammers and cranes, fewer construction workers are hired.

usiness investment hasn't grown for two years. Over the past two quarters, total business fixed investment has fallen by an annualized average of 4 percent. Business equipment and software has dropped by more than 5 percent. Non-residential structures — such as commercial office space, shopping malls, factories, and hotels — have dropped by nearly 8 percent.

But let's go further back. For the entire 32-quarter economic recovery, business fixed investment has averaged just 1.1 percent at an annual rate. Since 1960, however, business fixed investment has averaged 4.4 percent at an annual rate. So the present expansion in business investment is roughly one-quarter of the 55-year average.

Why? One key factor is tax policy, especially business tax policy.

At 40 percent for combined federal and state business tax rates, the U.S. has the largest corporate tax burden in the developed world. We double-tax corporate profits earned overseas, as virtually no other country does. Our depreciation rates for investment tax expensing are among the worst in the world. And despite all the talk about corporate tax reform, nothing gets done — even under a Republican Congress.

What's more, the Obama administration has raised tax rates on capital gains, dividends, and income (paid by small-business pass-throughs). So, as the tax cost of capital has gone up, business investment has come down.

Arthur Laffer has taught us: "If you tax something, you get less of it." That's why firms are moving offshore in droves. It's not about being unpatriotic. It's that it doesn't pay, after-tax, to invest in the United States.

A second key reason for the business-investment slump is monetary policy. While this may not be the right time for rate hikes, ultra-low interest rates have led to financial engineering rather than the deployment of excess corporate cash for productivity-enhancing investment.

Rather than invest in job creation and higher wages, firms are buying back stocks to boost price-earnings ratios. In many cases, they are even borrowing money they don't need so they can buy back stocks.

A third key reason for the business-investment collapse is over-regulation. Obamacare rules and mandates are job-killers. Dodd-Frank red-tape costs have held back lending to such an extent that business startups have practically come to a halt. And community banks have drastically pulled back loans to existing small businesses.

Then we have the Obama EPA's new rules, which amount to a war on fossil fuel. The president pushes for climate-change regulations instead of a massive build-out of energy infrastructure, including pipelines, liquid-natural-gas terminals and new refineries.

Want more manufacturing? The energy business, and the potential for North American energy independence, is the key. Hillary Clinton, with her promise to end oil and gas fracking, will pull us further in the wrong direction.

Many people do not understand that business investment is a critical prosperity-booster, leading to more jobs, higher wages, and stronger family income. Put another way, rising tax and regulatory burdens that penalize investors and businesses also punish middle-income wage earners.

And it's these wage earners who would benefit most from business tax reforms, such as a 15 percent corporate rate for large C-corps and small S-corps. This should be accompanied by immediate tax-deduction expensing for new investment and a territorial tax regime that would stop double-taxing profits earned abroad.

Study after study shows that corporate tax reform is a middle-class tax cut, not a tax cut for the rich. You see, corporations don't really pay taxes. They simply collect them and pass the cost along in the form of lower wages and benefits, higher consumer prices and reduced shareholder value.

The overarching theme of this election is an angry revolt by the middle class over the fact that jobs and wages have barely increased in the past decade. They blame Washington, China, immigration, power elites and almost everything else. So be it. There is a lot of work to be done on all these fronts. But without radical tax, regulatory and currency reform, business investment will never fully recover.

And neither will the economy.

Trump Must Prove That
He Can Do the Job

May 7, 2016

Donald Trump has swept the primaries and is now the presumptive GOP presidential nominee. His almost unbelievable primary surge — from New York to Indiana — was nothing short of breathtaking. He has confounded almost all the pundits and a majority of elected officials.

Going back to last summer, it was Trump's outsized political acumen that led him to understand the populist economic revolt that has been sweeping America. It's not just the anemic recovery under President Obama. It goes back 15 years, under Democratic and Republican administrations. The American economy has stalled. Middle-income wage earners have essentially had no pay increases since 2000. What's more, American foreign policy has gone off the rails.

And when Trump argued that America must become great again, whether at home or abroad, he hit a vein of political gold. And he got there before any of the other 16 GOP candidates.

This was a talented bunch — far better than anything the Democrats could produce. But Trump had the right instinct. He understood that the country wants someone who puts American interests first.

So he became the quintessential political outsider. It's what every Republican-primary exit poll showed that voters want. The people are in full revolt and will settle for nothing less than radical change in Washington, D.C., and the entire political system. That's what catapulted Trump to the nomination.

Now, Trump's critics in the GOP say he can't win in November. They say his candidacy will lead to a crushing Republican defeat — all the way down the ticket in state after state. Respectfully, I disagree.

Though it's early in the general-election process, a number of polls show Trump to be gaining significantly against Hillary Clinton. The RealClearPolitics polling average shows Trump only 6 or 7 percentage points back. And his general-election fight has barely begun.

All of this said, the single most important task ahead of Trump is to prove to Americans that he can do the job of president.

The people of this nation want a strong leader. They want someone who will crush ISIS. They want a fighter to sit across the table from Vladimir Putin. They want someone who can make the right trade deals with China, Japan and Mexico. They want someone to defend the southern border from illegal immigrants and ISIS intruders.

They also want someone to bring back the post-WWII prosperity, when America grew by 3.5 percent yearly on average, and when per capita GDP — a good measure of average wages — rose from $16,000 to nearly $50,000.

Knowing the two are intertwined, they want someone to bring both prosperity at home and peace abroad.

Trump must convince America he can do this. He must demonstrate a firm grasp of policies — on growth, jobs, wages, trade, immigration, foreign affairs and sound and stable money.

His speech before the American Israel Public Affairs Committee and his April foreign-policy address were successful serious speeches — teleprompter and all. He should replicate these. The economy, jobs, federal government spending, terrorism and immigration are the leading issues. Trump must speak to them. And when he makes his statements, he must stay on message, day after day.

I believe Trump's America-first, no-new-nation-building, destroy-ISIS ("Their days are numbered; I won't tell them where, and I won't tell them how. But they will be gone ... quickly") messaging is right on target.

He has a strong economic-growth plan. He just told CNBC, "We are lowering taxes very substantially and we're going to be getting rid of a tremendous amount of regulations."

On trade, he needs a coherent message that rules out protectionism. In his recent foreign-policy speech he talked up negotiations. The master of the art of the deal would be very good at that when it comes to trade. There's no need for huge tariffs. The goal here is to tear down *foreign* trade barriers and make China and others play by the rules.

And rather than trade wars and currency manipulation (which includes the U.S.), the world economic system should be anchored by stable and cooperative exchange-rate policies.

On immigration, Trump needs an articulate policy that aims to secure the border and keep out illegals while letting in skilled *legal* workers. Voters prefer a path to legality (not necessarily citizenship) rather than deportation. And Trump — a cost-conscious business executive — must translate that into curbing the cronyist federal-government leviathan.

There are other issues. But my key thought is that Trump can win by showing a consistent seriousness of purpose and demeanor, pro-growth economic policies and a more realistic national security strategy. He knows, as Ronald Reagan did, that success at home leads to success abroad.

Clinton is a weak candidate. Now Donald Trump must show that he can get the job done. He has the potential for great leadership. The whole world is watching. I believe he can do it.

Trump the Disrupter

May 14, 2016

Cathy McMorris Rodgers, the GOP House leadership member from Washington state, finally uttered the words I've been waiting to hear with respect to Donald Trump's march on the nation's capital. In an NBC News interview with my pal Luke Russert, she said that Trump is a "disrupter," and we have to learn that that's a good thing.

Perhaps because she's from Washington state, home to so many fabulous tech companies that disrupted the economy (Microsoft in its heyday, the all-powerful Amazon, and a laundry list that's too long for this column), she may understand the phenomenon more than anyone else in the GOP leadership.

New tech explosions create winners and losers, but overall are remarkably positive for the country, middle-class folks, the economy, jobs and wages. The trouble is, we haven't seen many disruptive tech breakthroughs lately. And maybe that's one reason why the economy is so sluggish.

But hats off to McMorris Rodgers for being the first member of the Republican leadership to understand that Trump, the ultimate outsider, is going to be a very disruptive force when he gets to Washington. And that's a good thing. It will finally re-launch America in a positive direction.

Now, I don't know if the Republican establishment is ready, but Trump has just had a very good week.

A bunch of polls show him running virtually even with Hillary Clinton nationwide and in key swing states, such as Florida, Pennsylvania and Ohio. Polls are not perfect, and it is still early in the November-election game, but the anti-Trump argument that

Trump and the Republican Party will be victims of a Hillary Clinton landslide is being put to rest.

And I think that's *one* reason why Trump's recent trip to Washington was such a success. The GOP may be breathing easier.

For Trump it was almost a listening tour. For the GOP leadership it was a get-to-know-you moment. And for Speaker Paul Ryan it was a chance to finally talk policy with the presumptive GOP nominee.

What I think I saw is that senior Republicans are deciding that it is better to help Trump than to harm him. Save the harm for Hillary Clinton, and help guide Trump to becoming an even stronger candidate.

Perhaps the major figure in all this was Ryan — one of the brightest of the bright and the biggest policy wonk of the wonks. He's also a classy guy, and he adopted a gracious posture toward Trump, even though he was not ready to endorse.

I wasn't in the room during that first meeting between Ryan and Trump. But reports suggest there was a good policy discussion. I'm going to guess that supply-side Ryan is fine with Trump's tax-cutting plan, designed to get the country out of a 15-year quagmire. And I think Ryan doesn't have much disagreement with Trump's deregulation instincts, though this plank has not been fleshed out. (I don't know if King Dollar currency stability came up.)

I also suspect Ryan will disagree with Trump on trade, where Trump has taken a hard line with China, Japan and other rule-breakers. And I gather Ryan has trouble with Trump's immigration plans to build a wall and deport illegal immigrants. Ryan has always been a free-trader and an immigration reformer, even while those positions are not so popular with the GOP anymore.

Finally, I'm going to conclude that Ryan has a problem with Trump's opposition to entitlement reform, including benefit cuts for Social Security and Medicare. Ryan of late has become a deficit and debt hawk, and apparently he came equipped for his Trump meeting with budget charts and slideshows. And while Trump shares Ryan's fears about future deficits and debt, he thus far is opposed to going after the big entitlements.

The gracious Speaker Ryan told the media that he can't decide everything in one 45-minute meeting. But he suggested the GOP "unity" process is advancing nicely. Ryan's lieutenants in the House

— Kevin McCarthy, Steve Scalise, and Greg Walden — have endorsed Trump, as has Mitch McConnell in the Senate. And Trump himself insists that his policy plans could be amended.

So I foresee an entente cordiale, which Webster's defines as a friendly understanding, especially between nations. (Of course everyone remembers the entente cordiale between Britain and France in 1904, mainly due to the diplomacy of King Edward VII!) In other words, Ryan and Trump can have a friendly relationship even while they disagree on some policies.

But here's the key point: Trump is not going to give up his economic populism or his America-first foreign policy. He has represented himself as the voice for the ailing American middle class. He *is* a disrupter. He will *always* be the outsider. And when elected he *will* follow through in Washington. Count on it.

Zuckerberg's Conservative Battle: Where There's Smoke, There's Fire

May 18, 2016

Mark Zuckerberg and his massive social-media site Facebook have come under strong criticism for allegedly suppressing stories of interest for conservative readers from its influential "trending" news section. Facebook has roughly 1.6 billion users worldwide, 167 million of whom are in the United States. Its "trending" section is therefore a powerful political influence.

Zuckerberg has denied the charges, and he will meet Wednesday with a handful of conservatives to discuss allegations that Facebook's "news curators" have manipulated its list of stories. The way it works at Facebook is that this powerful group of curators, or editors, who have access to a ranked list of trending topics generated by the company's algorithms, control the content of the trending-news section. In effect, these curators exercise gatekeeping powers, which amount to political news-making powers that are transmitted to Facebook's massive audience. Even The New York Times published an article this week titled "Social media finds new role as news and entertainment curator."

The anti-conservative curating bias was first reported by the tech blog Gizmodo. After that, a number of conservative outlets chimed in that the social-media giant has suppressed conservative views and related stories. This triggered news reports by the Wall Street Journal, the Guardian, The New York Times, and websites The Hill and Breitbart.

Among the conservatives slated to attend the Zuckerberg meeting are Glenn Beck, Dana Perino of Fox News, Arthur Brooks of the American Enterprise Institute, senior Donald Trump campaign aide Barry Bennett and former Romney digital director Zac Moffatt.

How these folks were picked for the meeting is anyone's guess. And what exactly is expected to come out of this meeting is unclear. It seems more like a public-relations gambit by Zuckerberg, who previously said Facebook will investigate all the conservative charges.

Curiously, last March, Zuckerberg gave a speech at a Facebook conference where he blasted Donald Trump and his policies. Also curious, Hillary Clinton, by a wide margin, has received the bulk of political donations from Facebook employees in this election cycle.

According to Breitbart, data from the Federal Election Commission show that Facebook staff gave $114,000 to Hillary Clinton. The next-closest recipient of political money was former Republican presidential candidate Marco Rubio. He only got $16,604.

Tom Stocky, the head of the trending-topics section at Facebook, maxed out with an individual donation of $2,700 to Hillary Clinton. The Hill website found that roughly 78 Facebook employees — from engineering, communications, public policy, strategy, marketing, human resources and other areas — donated to Clinton.

Meanwhile, Republican National Committee chairman Reince Priebus has tweeted, "Facebook must answer for conservative censorship." Sen. John Thune (R-S.D.), who is chairman of the Senate Committee on Commerce, warned Facebook of the need for consumer protection and an open Internet, and according to The Wall Street Journal Thune has sent a letter to Zuckerberg asking how the company chooses its trending topics and who is ultimately responsible. There are also a number of academics who have called for full transparency in the Facebook news process.

Of course, Facebook is a private company, and therefore is entitled to whatever political biases it holds. But given its gigantic scope and its power over so many people, and considering the mounting influence of all the social-media outlets, this is a very serious story.

We'll see what comes out of Wednesday's meeting. But as the American proverb goes: Where there's smoke, there's fire.

Are the Clintons the Real Housing-Crash Villains?

By Lawrence Kudlow and Stephen Moore
May 28, 2016

We are going to reveal the grand secret to getting rich by investing. It's a simple formula that has worked for Warren Buffett, Carl Icahn and all the greatest investment gurus over the years. Ready?

Buy low; sell high.

It turns out that Donald Trump has been very, very good at buying low and selling high, and it helps account for his amazing business success.

But now Hillary Clinton seems to think it's a crime. Campaigning in California last week she wailed that Trump "actually said he was hoping for the crash that caused hardworking families in California and across America to lose their homes, all because he thought he could take advantage of it to make some money for himself." She's assailing Trump for being a good businessman — something she would know almost nothing about, because she's never actually run a business, though she did miraculously turn $1,000 into $100,000 in the cattle futures market many years ago.

Clinton's new TV ads say that Trump predicted the real estate crash in 2006 (good call) and then bought real estate at low prices when the housing crash, which few others foresaw, came in 2008. Many builders went out of business during the crash, but Trump read the market perfectly.

What is so hypocritical about the Clinton attacks is that it wasn't Trump but Hillary Clinton, her husband and many of her biggest supporters who were the real culprits here.

Before Clinton is able to rewrite this history, let's look at the many ways the Clintons and cronies contributed to the Great Recession.

The seeds of the mortgage meltdown were planted during Bill Clinton's presidency.

Under Andrew Cuomo, Clinton's secretary of Housing and Urban Development, Community Reinvestment Act regulators gave banks higher ratings for home loans made in credit-deprived areas. Banks were effectively rewarded for throwing out sound underwriting standards and writing loans to those who were at high risk of defaulting. If banks didn't comply with these rules, regulators reined in their ability to expand lending and deposits.

These new HUD rules lowered down payments from the traditional 20 percent to 3 percent by 1995 and zero down payments by 2000. What's more, in the Clinton push to issue home loans to lower-income borrowers, Fannie and Freddie made it a common practice to virtually end credit documentation, low credit scores were disregarded and income and job history was also thrown aside. The phrase "subprime" became commonplace. What an understatement.

Next the Clinton administration's rules ordered the taxpayer-backed Fannie Mae and Freddie Mac to expand their quotas of risky loans from 30 percent of portfolio to 50 percent, as part of a big push to expand home ownership. Fannie and Freddie were securitizing these home loans and offering 100 percent taxpayer guarantees of repayment. So now taxpayers were on the hook for these risky, low down payment loans.

Tragically, when prices fell, lower income folks who really could not afford these mortgages under normal credit standards suffered massive foreclosures and personal bankruptcies. Many will never get credit again. It's a perfect example of liberals using government allegedly to help the poor, with the ultimate consequences being disastrous to them.

Additionally, ultra-easy money from the Federal Reserve also played a key role. Rates were held too low for too long from 2002 through 2005, which created asset price bubbles in housing, commodities, gold, oil and elsewhere. When the Fed finally tightened, prices collapsed. So did mortgage collateral (homes) and mortgage bonds that depended on the collateral. Many bond packages were written to please Fannie and Freddie, based on the fantastical idea that home prices would never fall. Fannie and Freddie, by the way, cost the taxpayers $187 billion.

Just to make this story worse, Sen. Hillary Clinton and Sen. Barack Obama voted to filibuster a Republican effort to roll back Fannie and Freddie. But on top of all this, while Clinton was propping up Fannie and Freddie, she was taking contributions from their foundations, as a Washington Times report concluded.

"Freddie Mac and Fannie Mae's political action committee and individuals linked to the companies donated $75,500 to Mrs. Clinton's senatorial campaign," according to the Washington Times. "Freddie Mac also gave the Clinton Foundation a $50,000 to $100,000 donation."

To be clear, there was plenty of blame to go around among both political parties and the horde of housing lobbyists who helped set up this real estate house of cards. It's a sordid story with plenty of blame all around. And the Fannie/Freddie story is still not solved. It now includes profit sweeping from shareholders to the government, thereby ending any chance to sell the mortgage agencies back to the private sector.

Meanwhile, Clinton's attempt to blame Donald Trump is utterly absurd. Buying low and selling high is not against the law. In fact, Trump's investment acumen may serve America well in the not-too-distant future.

A Business Recession Looms

June 4, 2016

The U.S. Bureau of Labor Statistics May job report was a shocker, with nonfarm payrolls up only 38,000 and private jobs up a mere 25,000. A lot of investors and economists are making the case that this was a weird, one-off statistical glitch, and that stronger employment is on the way. They may very well be wrong.

If you smooth out the numbers by looking at a three-month moving average, job increases have been slowing for five months. The three-month pace last December was 281,000 jobs. Since then, the pace has nosedived to 107,000. The unemployment rate fell to 4.7 percent, but that's largely because 458,000 people left the labor force.

This spells trouble for the economy. And if you step back and look at the whole business sector, a case can be made that the U.S. has been in a mild business recession for as much as a year, if not longer.

Take, for example, fixed investment in equipment, software, plants, buildings and so forth. This has been slowing for six straight quarters and even went negative in the first quarter on a year-to-year basis.

Behind this business-investment slowdown, the broadest measure of profits from the gross domestic product accounts, which very closely tracks IRS profits, has been negative for the past three quarters measured year to year. In fact, this slump began in the second half of 2014, almost two years ago.

Profits are the mother's milk of stocks and the lifeblood of the economy. While so many people obsess about the Federal Reserve, the reality is that stocks have been flat over the past year as profits and business investment have weakened.

Another point: Core capital goods, including orders, shipments and backlogs, have turned negative over the past three months, and over the past year. This is a proxy for business investment, and it's not a good omen.

Finally, the closely watched Institution for Supply Management reports for manufacturing and services show a PMI barely above 50 percent. In other words, they point to the front end of a recession. On the manufacturing side, key indicators like production and employment are below year-ago levels. New orders are flat. On the services side, the overall index is below year-ago levels, as is employment and new orders.

Many financial folks concentrate on consumption rather than business indicators, clinging to an outdated view that consumers are 70 percent of the U.S. economy. To be sure, consumer spending and housing are rising modestly. But new research by economist Dr. Mark Skousen of Chapman University shows that if you look under the hood of the GDP accounts, you will find that the intermediate stages of business production and services, including business-to-business activity, account for 50 percent of overall output. That's higher than consumption, which runs about 40 percent.

As a result of Skousen's work, the U.S. Bureau of Economic Analysis has created a new "gross output" measure, which is published with a lag. The GO measurement tells us a lot more about the inside workings of the economy. And according to Skousen, 80 percent of all employment actually comes in the early and intermediate stages of business activity.

So let this be a warning. The overall economy is not yet in recession; but the business economy has been slipping for quite some time. And if falling profits and business investment continues, the job slowdown will follow suit — if it hasn't already.

As for Fed watching, in this environment, the Fed should stay put. No rate hikes. The time for raising target rates was back in 2011, when the second round of quantitative easing drove the Consumer Price Index up to 3.8 percent. That's when it should have increased the target rate by a percentage point or so. If it had, it would have gotten back to Stanford economist John Taylor's rule. We would have all been better off for it.

But now is the time to turn away from monetary policy and focus instead on fiscal solutions for the ailing economy. Slashing business tax rates to 15 percent for large and small companies and overturning burdensome regulations is what the economy needs to get out of the doldrums.

That would bring business investment back. The U.S. would be the most hospitable investment destination in the world. America would win the global race for capital. Cash would be put to work in productivity-enhancing investments. And the economy would grow by 4 or 5 percent for years.

Real interest rates reflecting higher economic returns would rise as a sign of economic health. And then the Fed could normalize its policies by following market rates higher.

For a time, the dollar would jump, again reflecting market forces and not currency manipulation. Then the G-20, with strong U.S. leadership for a change, could coordinate currency values and stability.

That's my vision. Alas, we're going to have to wait until next year.

Overthrow the Establishment to Fix the Economy

June 15, 2016

Famed investor Wilbur Ross recently told CNBC that "Trump represents a more radical new approach to government that the nation's economy desperately needs." He's right. Trump seeks an overthrow of the establishment. He's a disrupter — just what we need to fix the economy.

The situation is that desperate.

The last 15 years of economic policy, especially the last eight years, represent a relapse that harks back to the 1970s. Now, like then, we have a policy mix of high taxation, high spending, high regulation, priming of the Fed pump, manipulation of the dollar and no standard. In general, it's a government-planning approach in the U.S. and around the world.

We've not experienced high inflation in recent years, but that's not because the Fed hasn't tried hard enough. Meanwhile, all the quantitative easing, bond buying and interest-rate fixing did not succeed.

It's been a Keynesian mishmash. Gigantic federal spending and infrastructure building (remember "shovel ready" jobs?). Overtaxed investors, successful earners, and large and small businesses. Overregulated banks, energy resources, businesses and health care. None of it worked. Whatever happened to those government-spending multipliers? They never happened.

The economy has barely recovered from the so-called Great Recession, with a 2 percent annual growth rate since mid-2009. Peak worker wages, business investment and productivity all occurred around the year 2000.

The U.S. has the highest corporate tax system in the world, companies and their cash are fleeing overseas, welfare rolls are skyrocketing, employment participation rates are falling and interest-rate markets have come under the spell of the Fed's misallocation of credit.

And in response to all that, the general electorate — the middle class in particular — is angry and suffering high anxiety about the future.

As American Enterprise Institute President Arthur C. Brooks argues, people who earn their own income are happy campers, while people who live on government assistance are unhappy. So, at the margin, if you count more people living off government welfare assistance, and even those working who are earning less in real inflation-adjusted terms, it's a very unhappy country.

Putting aside the growing threat of Islamic jihadi terrorism, most of America's problems are homegrown. So when I say overthrow the establishment to fix the economy, and the brilliant businessman Ross says we need radical new approaches to government, we're talking two sides of the same coin.

In the 1980s and 1990s, radical change in economic policies fostered by U.S. President Ronald Reagan and British Prime Minister Margaret Thatcher put the brakes on government planning and ushered in a new free-market, supply-side era and a two-decade boom. That model has been abandoned in the new century. This must be reversed.

Who, exactly, do I mean by the establishment that needs overthrowing? Much of the blame must be placed on the high-pedigreed economists inside and outside government who advise politicians, policymakers, the Fed, big corporate CEOs and interest-group trade associations to pursue a cronyist corporate-welfare system that both creates and then relies on a government-driven economy. I don't mean all economists; there are still a few free-marketeers out there.

And while Democratic policy planners are the vanguard of the new Bernie Sanders democratic socialism — with Hillary Clinton right in the pack — many Republican advisors are also to blame.

Now, Trump may be an imperfect candidate in his rookie political season, but he gets the basic economic story right: Lower taxes, especially large- and small-business taxes. Roll back regulations. Make use of all forms of energy. Take a market-oriented and consumer-choice approach to health care and education. Have a friendly attitude toward entrepreneurs.

If Trump follows through with his free-market-oriented policy direction, the American economy will take off like a rocket.

Growth is the key, not inequality. Growth creates new businesses, new jobs, higher wages and a stronger middle class. Growth eases the burdens of poverty. Growth makes everyone happier.

But today, not surprisingly, the business sector is slipping into recession. Profits, production, investment, core capital goods and business equipment have gone negative. Since supply creates its own demand, the slump in business could spread to the consumer — unless policies are turned around.

Pre-election, that won't happen. Post-election, it just might. But that's at least six months away.

And the irony of ironies: A bumbling Fed made the right decision to back off interest-rate hikes. In fact, the real message of rock-bottom rates around the world is stagnation and deflation.

But global central banks, much like their governments, are a long stone's throw away from sound money and currency stabilization. It's just like our errant fiscal policies.

To save the economy, things must change.

"You only get to vote for who's on the ballot paper, and your choices are between Hillary Clinton and Donald Trump, and I find that an easy choice to make," said Ross.

By the way, business titan Wilbur Ross would make a very good Treasury secretary, wouldn't he?

Magna Carta 2.0: Good for Freedom, Good for Growth

June 25, 2016

The original Magna Carta was a charter agreed upon by King John of England in 1215. Its 801st anniversary just passed. So no, I wasn't there. But that charter has become part of an important, iconic and political myth that the deal between an unpopular king and rebellious barons marked the beginning of individual English freedoms, personal liberties and due-process protection of individuals under the law. The Magna Carta has also been cited as providing the essential foundation for the contemporary powers of Parliament and legal principles such as habeas corpus.

That's the mythology, and it's important.

While I understand that describing the Brexit victory as Magna Carta 2.0 is inexact, I think it makes a key point: Britain will regain its political freedom, its autonomous self-government and its independence from an EU that is spinning out of control under the power of establishment elites, unelected and unaccountable socialist bureaucrats, and a judicial court that is increasingly making legal decisions that replace Britain's powerful common law.

The EU's tax and regulatory policies, climate-change and welfare spending and free immigration — even in wartime — are gradually ruining Europe. That's why I believe Brexit is good for British freedom, political autonomy and the survival of democratic capitalism.

The business elites told British voters that leaving the EU would lead to economic catastrophe. Well, in England, Main Street defeated the establishment elites by sending a populist message.

And there need be no economic catastrophe. The EU needs Britain more than Britain needs the EU. The London Stock Exchange is one of the most powerful financial centers in the world. The Frankfurt Stock Exchange will never replace it.

Trade is the key to the economic outlook in Britain and the EU. Many corporate chieftains joined large-bank CEOs and the fearmongering International Monetary Fund to suggest that the EU will deal harshly with Britain and stop all trade if it leaves. That's mutually assured destruction — MAD. A tariff-driven trade war would destroy both power centers.

Not only does the EU need Britain's financial capabilities. Britain itself is a major importer of EU goods and services. If sanity prevails, there's no reason why the EU and Britain can't hammer out a free-trade agreement in the two years allotted by the Lisbon Treaty.

And if the EU wants to go with MAD, the whole setup will burn in flames.

Yes, there's a lot of disagreement about the economic consequences of Brexit. But remember that Britain is still a member of the IMF, the World Bank, G-7, G-20, the WTO, NATO and so on.

Veteran Wall Street economist Robert Sinche wrote a note to clients in the early evening of the vote saying that there was a high probability that Brexit would win. He wrote, "Most analysts have overestimated the negative impact of a leave vote as the UK has been a marginal member of the EU on/off for many decades." Brave chap. But I agree.

And we should also remember that the Bank of England — a better operation than the European Central Bank — will still be in business, as will the British pound sterling.

My advice to investors is to ride out the short-term market volatility, which may last several months, and look instead at the long-term positives of political and economic freedom.

It will now be up to Boris Johnson, the likely new British prime minster, and the Tory party, perhaps with bipartisan help, to negotiate a good trade deal and move more aggressively on the pro-growth path of free-market supply-side policies.

There's already talk about abolishing the 5 percent value added tax on household energy. Good. Taxes need to be reduced across the board, heavy regulations need to be rolled back and government spending needs to be restrained.

This is Britain's opportunity. It's kind of a Thatcher moment.

If you look under the hood of the populist revolt in Britain and the budding revolts in larger Europe and America, the anger is in good part rooted in the lack of economic, job and wage growth. Worldwide, growth has been missing. All the major countries have been operating under big-government spending, heavy regulations and the insane central-bank policies of QE and zero (now negative) interest rates. It hasn't worked. Middle-income wage earners have had enough.

Plus, wartime immigration policies have been too easy. And the major countries, including America, have not destroyed ISIS. So this popular revolt is also aimed at national-security failures.

The American election in November may parallel the British story. President Barack Obama, who insulted British voters by campaigning in London against Brexit, is a huge loser. Hillary Clinton will suffer from this. Donald Trump will benefit.

So I'll end where I began: Brexit is good for freedom, growth and Britain. Ride out short-term financial and economic volatility. And watch for a full populist revolt in America this fall.

Trump's Two Homers: Pence and Promise for a Declaration of War

June 16, 2016

Donald Trump hit two home runs this week. The first, immediately following the horrific terrorist truck attack in Nice, was his statement in a media interview wherein he said that if elected, he would ask Congress for a declaration of war to combat global terrorism. The second was the inspired selection of Indiana governor Mike Pence to join the GOP ticket.

Before getting to Pence, let me linger a moment on Trump's declaration-of-war pronouncement.

For well over a year, I have argued for a Washington wake-up call whereby the president and Congress enact a formal declaration of war against ISIS and all other Islamic jihadist terror groups. These groups have declared war on us. We have yet to respond.

Following the tragic terrorist attacks in Paris late last year, French president Francois Hollande declared war on ISIS. It was an act of courage. But France had to go it alone.

France has been an American ally for about 250 years. It is a key member of NATO. But President Obama never stood shoulder to shoulder with Hollande and asked for a declaration of war against ISIS. Nor did he use American clout for a NATO declaration of war.

Why is this important? I believe a war declaration would show energy, urgency, determination and leadership — not only to rally Americans, but to send a global message to the terrorists.

I recently interviewed former secretaries of state Henry Kissinger and George P. Shultz, as well as retired four-star general Jack Keane.

They all endorsed a full-throated U.S. declaration of war. And they added that with such a declaration, the U.S. must be prepared to destroy ISIS in its safe havens in Iraq and Syria.

So when Donald Trump made it clear that this, in fact, "is war," deserving of a declaration of war, he distinguished himself. No one else has done it. Not Congress. Not Obama. Certainly not Clinton.

Trump's second home run was his selection of Mike Pence as his running mate. Down through the years, as a leader of the conservative House Republican Study Committee and later as the third-ranking member of the House Republican leadership team, he stood firm as a genuine and consistent conservative.

On economic policy Pence has held to the key building block of growth. He is a budget hawk who voted against President George W. Bush's fiscally bloated No Child Left Behind education bill and hyper-expensive Medicare prescription-drug bill. He said he would not support new middle-class entitlements. He was consistent.

Just over 10 years ago, Pence was voted conservative man of the year by Human Events. I did the interview and subsequent write-up. Pence described himself as "an unregenerate supply-sider" whose central aim is to marry supply-side tax cuts with strict spending restraint to expand the economy and get the budget into balance.

A few years ago, Pence spoke to the Detroit Economic Club. He called for sound monetary reform, tax relief, access to American energy, regulatory reform, and trade. New York Sun editor Seth Lipsky reminds us that Trump has stood for a stable and reliable dollar, including a standard to back it up. Pence stands for these same things.

In Indiana, which has been hard hit by manufacturing losses, job declines and shrinking wages, Governor Pence combined tax cuts with spending restraint to spur the Hoosier economy. In this important respect he would be an excellent spokesman within the industrial Rust Belt, which includes Iowa, Michigan, Ohio and Pennsylvania. These states have all suffered similarly, but they're states where polling suggests Trump could carry the day in November. Pence helps get him there.

Contributing to GOP unity, Pence is a churchgoing evangelical family man. He believes that "the sanctity of human life is the central axiom of Western civilization." In this respect he will be an important bridge to social conservatives. And he might just soften the opposition of the Never Trump movement.

And Pence is well acquainted with the ways of Washington. He has strong ties to Speaker Paul Ryan and he is well regarded by GOP leaders in both the Senate and the House.

Finally, he will prove to be a tough and unyielding spokesman for the Trump ticket. Pence is a fighter. He will happily go after Clinton's awful record.

So this was a week where we learned a Trump-Pence ticket will seek to declare and wage war to destroy ISIS. We learned that the GOP ticket is pro-growth, ready for tax cuts and deregulation. And we learned that the ticket will be allied with traditional and social conservatives. With these credentials, Trump-Pence is in position to carry states in November that no Republican has won in decades.

It was also a week where Clinton's polls were like stocks looking for a bottom. Trump-Pence is a winner for the GOP.

Pence Saves Republican
Party After Cruz Disaster

July 22, 2016

Ted Cruz essentially gave a career-ending speech at the GOP convention on Wednesday night.

Cruz's speech was a slap in the face to GOP nominee Donald Trump. "Vote your conscience" is a wonderful-sounding phrase. But we all know what he meant: Don't vote for Donald Trump.

I was in the convention hall and the crowd's reaction was unbelievable. It started out as a few hands waving in the air and some booing, and then it just grew and grew throughout the entire convention hall. And then boom! It was absolute bedlam.

I've been to most of the GOP conventions since 1980, and I've never seen anything like it. These people stood on their feet and booed. These are Republicans! They don't do this. They don't know how to stand up and boo. And yet, Cruz so divided them and worked them into such frenzy that it happened.

Cruz tried to pass it off as just the New York delegation acting up. But that is wrong. The whole hall was in an uproar. You couldn't even hear the last two paragraphs of Cruz's speech because the booing had reached such a crescendo.

Cruz left an absolute disaster in his wake when he finished that speech. Everyone was dispirited, as one might expect.

And then came Trump's running mate, Mike Pence. Pence delivered a terrific speech. He touched on all the major themes — the economy, shaking up Washington and Trump's outsider roots. He talked about how Trump understands that middle-class wage earners have been hurt; they haven't had a raise in 15 years. That's something that Cruz, in all of his years of political experience, still doesn't understand!

Really, within the first 10 minutes of his speech, Mike Pence turned a demoralized, dispirited, depressed, negative convention into an upbeat and united one. He hit all the right notes and had a lot of optimism in his speech. The Cruz disaster, which had left the convention hall spinning just moments before, was suddenly swept away.

The entire hall started applauding Pence. Then they started cheering and got on their feet for Pence. Amazing.

Trump couldn't have made a better choice. Mike Pence single-handedly pulled the convention back together and united attendees with an optimistic message. He gave great support to Donald Trump and the ticket. He basically snatched victory from the jaws of defeat. He turned destruction into positive hope.

I've never seen anything like that.

Ted Cruz will never politically recover from this. His delegation from Texas wanted him to play ball with Trump — and he wouldn't. He was freelancing in that speech. His political career is over. He's finished.

Donald Trump and Mike Pence are just beginning.

We have to wait and see what Trump does tonight in his speech; it could make or break his presidential campaign. I personally hope that he puts a lot of focus on positive changes for America. I want to see a lot of growth in that speech. I want to hear him talk about lowering taxes and curbing regulations.

But here's what I want to see most of all: a follow-through from what Pence started. One of Pence's messages on Wednesday night was that we — meaning the ticket — can turn this nation around. It's an American malaise right now, from the economy, to civil unrest, violence and the threat of terrorism. And that is what Trump must prove to the nation and the world — that he can turn it around. He's got to convince them.

It's kind of like Ronald Reagan redux. Reagan was able to do this. He proved that he could do the job. That's what Trump needs to do.

That's huge. It's more important than any policy detail.

And that's the spirit Pence invoked on Wednesday night. Let's hope Trump does the same.

The Hillary Clinton Recession

July 30, 2016

This economy may be perilously close to recession. That was the message of the second-quarter real GDP report and its meager 1.2 percent growth rate.

Over the past year, real GDP has slipped to a paltry 1.2 percent. Business investment continues to fall. Building and factory construction has dropped sharply. Productivity is flat. The profits recession is still in force.

And what's the Hillary Clinton plan? Tax us into prosperity.

In her own words at the Democratic National Convention in Philadelphia on Thursday night, Clinton said, "Wall Street, corporations, and the super-rich are going to start paying their fair share of taxes." That's her fix. Why? She continued: "Not because we resent success. Because when more than 90 percent of gains have gone to the top 1 percent, that's where the money is."

Let me get this right. In order to spur growth, Clinton intends to raise taxes on individuals, businesses, capital gains, stock trading and firms that move overseas (which they do because the U.S. has the most uncompetitive tax system in the corporate world)? In addition, Clinton's door is open for a carbon tax, higher payroll taxes and a 25 percent gun tax.

She also argued in Philadelphia that the economy is not working the way it should because our democracy isn't working the way it should.

Huh.

What she's getting at is appointing Supreme Court justices who "will get money out of politics" and pass "a constitutional amendment to overturn Citizens United."

Citizens United removed spending limits for super-PACs. And yet those mean and nasty super-PACs have thus far benefited from pro-Clinton hedge fund contributions to the tune of $48.5 million, according to the Wall Street Journal.

Donald Trump, on the other hand, has received only $19,000 from hedge funds.

Get it? Citizens United, according to Clinton, is the source of our weak recovery and it must be overturned. Meanwhile, she is the big beneficiary of the Supreme Court decision to allow unlimited political donations.

Next, there are the recurring themes of class warfare and inequality, roots of evil according to Clinton. Turns out that the top 1 percent received a big share of income growth during the recovery. OK, but it also suffered the biggest loss during the Great Recession.

Research from Scott Winship of the Manhattan Institute shows that during the recession, the top 1 percent lost 36 percent of its income while the bottom 90 percent lost 12 percent. Through 2014 the top 1 percent was still poorer by 18 percent than it was in 2000. That's compared to a 9 percent decline for the rest of us.

According to Winship, income for the top 1 percenters was basically no higher in 2014 than in 2000. It turns out that that group bumped into the same income stagnation suffered by the U.S. middle class since 2000.

And according to new studies by Aparna Mathur of American Enterprise Institute, raising top marginal tax rates reduces growth incentives and yields very few revenues. Yet, in addition to higher tax rates, Clinton wants $1 trillion in new spending programs.

The numbers also don't add up for President Obama, who defended his so-called recovery at the DNC and even called Clinton a 30-year member of the establishment, a change-maker.

Obama's seven-year recovery averaged 2.1 percent real growth at an annualized rate. For historical comparison, after seven years, President John F. Kennedy's economy increased by 5.4 percent yearly and President Ronald Reagan's by 4.5 percent.

Did Kennedy and Reagan beget long booms by raising taxes? No. They cut tax rates across the board.

Clinton is a combination of Barack Obama 3.0 and Bernie Sanders 2.0. This is not change. This will not yield strong growth, lift jobs and wages, and make America more globally competitive.

A week prior to the DNC Trump offered a different perspective at the Republican National Convention: "America is one of the highest-taxed nations in the world. Reducing taxes will cause new companies and new jobs to come roaring back into our country. ... Then we are going to deal with the issue of regulation, one of the greatest job-killers of them all. ... We are going to lift restrictions on the production of American energy. ... With these new economic policies, trillions and trillions of dollars will start flowing into our country."

So Trump wants to reduce tax rates and regulations, unleash energy and make America the most hospitable investment destination in the world. Clinton wants to raise taxes, regulations and spending and put the energy sector out of business. (She would abolish coal and oil-and-gas fracking.)

No wonder the blue-collar, hard-hat, Democrat middle class is going for Trump.

Clinton is not an agent of change, nor does she have any idea how to restore rapid economic growth. Instead, she is a prisoner of the left.

If Trump stays on his growth message, he'll whup her in November.

Donald Trump Is the Middle-Class Growth Candidate

August 9, 2016

Did Hillary Clinton actually propose raising middle-income taxes in a recent speech? The audio suggests she said, "We are going to raise taxes on the middle class," although the prepared remarks indicate she meant, "We aren't going to." Well, these things happen. But the fact remains that Clinton's proposals to raise taxes on so-called rich people, rich corporations, Wall Street, investors (capital gains, dividends and financial transactions) and estates will greatly harm middle-income wage earners, who have essentially not had a pay raise since the year 2000.

Donald Trump gave a major economic speech in Detroit, Michigan, on Monday. In general terms, he will be lowering marginal tax rates for large and small businesses and all income classes. He also proposed a hike in the standard deduction for families, as well as special deductions for childcare.

All of these polices will help the middle class. Trump's plan will generate substantial new investment, business formation, jobs and growth — and hence, higher wages.

Trump is the pro-growth candidate in this race. Clinton is the anti-growth candidate. Trump wants to expand national income and the economic pie. Clinton wants to redistribute income and shrink the pie.

In past writings, I have equated Trump's tax-reduction plan to the John F. Kennedy and Ronald Reagan tax cuts, which generated economic booms of roughly 5 percent growth per year. President

Obama, by comparison, has raised taxes, spending and regulations, producing the worst recovery since World War II. And Clinton intends to follow in Obama's footsteps, with a Bernie Sanders-like, left-wing policy mix. She is the Democrats' anti-JFK. What a pity.

I want to draw on some academic work to validate how Trump is the pro-growth, pro-middle-class candidate.

Let me begin with American Enterprise Institute economists Aparna Mathur and Kevin Hassett. They have written extensively on the adverse effects of high corporate taxes on worker wages. They argue that high taxes drive capital out of the high-tax country, like the U.S., which leads to lower domestic investment. That, in turn, reduces the productivity of the worker, who will lack the latest advances in technology and machinery. And since there is a tight link between worker productivity and pay, lower wages result.

Mathur and Hassett cite famous University of Chicago economist Arnold Harberger to explain that when taxes are raised on corporations wages are lowered not only for the workers in those firms, but for all workers in the economy. So, a $1 corporate income tax leads to a $1 loss in wages for a firm's workers. But that tax could lead to more than a $1 loss overall, when we look at wages for all workers.

Obama and Clinton wrongly believe that the corporate income tax is a tax on the rich. The reality is that rich corporations don't pay taxes — workers do.

Another erroneous claim from Obama and Clinton is that the rich don't pay their fair share. But a new Congressional Budget Office study shows that the so-called rich pay the lion's share of federal taxes. It revealed that in 2013 the top 1 percent of households paid an average of 34 percent of income in federal taxes, while the middle 20 percent of households paid only 12.8 percent. This was confirmed by a recent Tax Foundation report.

And taxes for the top 1 percent have been going up. According to the report, Between 2008 and 2012, the top 1 percent paid an average tax rate of 28.8 percent. But in 2013 that rate spiked to 34 percent as a result of tax increases and the Affordable Care Act. This data is summarized by Mark J. Perry of the University of Michigan and AEI.

It's also worth noting that the so-called rich haven't had it so great lately. Recent studies by Manhattan Institute economist Scott Winship and Cato Institute economist Alan Reynolds show that during the Great Recession the top 1 percent lost 36 percent of its income, while income for the bottom 90 percent lost 12 percent. As of 2014, the top 1 percent was still 18 percent poorer than it was in 2007, compared with a 9 percent decline for the bottom 90 percent. Reynolds also notes that middle-incomes fell only 1 percent during the 2007-09 recession, after counting tax cuts and government benefits.

These facts and figures slay a lot of left-wing urban legends — highly divisive urban legends, I might add.

What matters most for all Americans is economic growth. As Arthur Laffer frequently reminds us: Tax something more, get less of it. Tax something less, get more of it.

Trump's big-bang economic speech outlines policies to tax growth less and restore American prosperity. Clinton, on the other hand, has nothing but prosperity killers up her sleeve.

Insanity Once More:
The Hillary Clinton Economic Plan

August 16, 2016

Doing the same thing over and over again and expecting different results, when in fact the results never change, is one definition of insanity. That goes for economics, too.

Over the past seven and a half years, President Obama has maintained a steady course of burdensome new regulations, significant tax increases and massive federal spending on so-called infrastructure. He has unconstitutionally ordered executive actions, favored labor over business, attacked banks, insulted successful corporate leaders and backed federal government mandates on business.

And with all this, strong economic recovery from a deep recession — which has been an American tradition — never came to pass.

A recent Wall Street Journal news headline read, "The Worst Expansion Since World War II Was Even Weaker." The story proclaimed that this lackluster economic expansion is actually getting weaker.

Another recent Journal column titled "Productivity Slump Threatens Economy's Long-Term Growth" asserted that output per hour is experiencing the longest losing streak since 1979. The U-6 unemployment rate stands twice as high as the traditional unemployment rate, the U-3.

Yet Obama has continued to do the same thing over and over again.

And now comes Hillary Clinton's economic plan, which will deliver more stagnant growth, falling wages, dropping productivity and depressed investment.

Her program would raise the estate tax and taxes on so-called rich people, corporations, capital gains and stock transactions. She would spend massively on infrastructure and again mandate rules for private businesses. Remarkably, she has no corporate tax reform (even Obama had a plan) to revive corporate investment and boost productivity, wages and living standards.

Now, here's the question: By repeating Obama's policies, how does she expect the economy to do any better than it has during his presidency?

She doesn't.

Clinton's goal is not economic growth but reducing inequality and social injustice in the name of "fairness." But she never tells us what "fair" means, although we know it's code for higher taxes and larger government.

Let's bring in Donald Trump. He wants to lower taxes across the board for individuals and large and small businesses, significantly reduce burdensome regulations and unleash America's energy resources. (Clinton would end coal and fracking.) Trump's corporate tax reform would restore America's position as the most hospitable investment climate in the world. For a change, businesses and their cash would come back home.

The contrast between the two economic-policy strategies couldn't be clearer. Clinton has a recession strategy; Trump has a recovery strategy.

Clinton derides Trump's plan as more "trickle-down economics." But she forgets something. Post-war economies prospered most following President John F. Kennedy's and President Ronald Reagan's tax cuts. In fact, in his second term, President Bill Clinton followed the incentive model of growth by reducing taxes and reforming welfare, with excellent economic results.

So why not give tax and regulatory relief a try? It's been missing for seven and a half years. Why not do something different for a change?

When you read Hillary Clinton's Detroit economic speech you see repeated references to making sure the top 1 percent pays its fair share. Ditto for corporations.

But here's a big factual mistake. A recent CBO study shows that "'the rich' don't just pay a 'fair share' of federal taxes, they pay almost everybody's share," particularly when it comes to financing government transfer payments.

A recent Tax Foundation study using IRS data shows that in 2013 the top 1 percent paid an average 34 percent of federal taxes, while the middle 20 percent paid only 12.8 percent.

What's more, numerous studies show that cutting business taxes will benefit wage earners the most. That's the middle class.

Yes, shareholder stock values will go up, too. But it's not simply the rich who gain from this. Remember, all those government and private-sector unions are heavily invested in stocks. They hate tax cuts. But it is precisely those tax cuts that will boost their pension and retirement-benefit totals. Ironic, isn't it?

Plainly, Trump intends to reward success, while Clinton will punish it. She wants the government to run the economy. He believes in the growth engine of free enterprise.

Trump understands that you can't have good-paying jobs unless you have strong, healthy businesses. But if investors and businesses are harassed by overregulation and uncompetitive taxes, firms will stagnate or fail, and jobs and wages will shrink.

Clinton never ran a business, so she doesn't understand this model. It's not a Republican or Democratic model. It's a common-sense, American model of prosperity.

A long time ago, I watched President Reagan repeat a few simple points about the benefits for everyone of lower taxes, light regulations and limited government. Successful policies are sold by repetition, not unrelated tangents. Trump must learn this. If he does he will win. But if he doesn't Americans will continue to suffer. We'll have more of the same bad policies and more of the same bad results.

Insanity.

Hillary Clinton, You're No John F. Kennedy

September 3, 2016

The election season is heating up. Donald Trump has pulled back even with Hillary Clinton, and every new economic number is being scrutinized for its supposed political meaning.

The unexpectedly soft U.S. Bureau of Labor Statistics August job report will lend a little political advantage to Trump. In general, jobs came in 30,000 to 40,000 below expectations. Manufacturing and goods-producing jobs decreased, wages were nearly flat and retreated to 2.4 percent year on year, the private and manufacturing workweeks fell, and overall hours dropped.

However, this is far from a catastrophe. Jobs still climbed by 150,000 or so. And the third-quarter ending in September will probably generate a near-3 percent growth as inventories reverse course and start rising again. These numbers may well lend some political advantage to Clinton.

But if you look under the economy's hood, you'll discover a business recession that has been going on for quite a while. Profits, productivity, business investment and Institute for Supply Management manufacturing are all down. According to Chapman University Professor Dr. Mark Skousen, business-to-business supply-chain activity — which hardly anyone looks at — has been hurting for well over a year. And bank loans are in a slump.

If these trends continue, jobs and wages will continue to slip.

So, what's to be done?

Well, if you have a business recession, which could easily spread to consumers, the policy fix has nothing to do with whether or not the Fed raises its target rate by a quarter point. Nothing.

Instead, the trick is to help business with new incentives. And that's why I have been for Trump's tax-reform plan since last winter.

Trump aims to slash business tax rates to 15 percent for large and small firms, allow for immediate write-offs for new investment and enact a sensible repatriation plan to bring a couple trillion dollars in cash back to America.

He also wants to lighten regulatory overload — in particular getting rid of Obamacare — and loosen bank credit for Main Street.

If he is able to put all this together, it would be the single biggest stimulant for middle-income wage earners in a very long time.

Want to raise wages? Slash business taxes. Want to help business get out of recession and into recovery? Then help business.

For the life of me, I cannot understand Clinton and her proposed across-the-board tax hikes on individuals, businesses and investors. I cannot fathom her plans for increased regulatory burdens, which include more government-run healthcare and a halt to the fossil-fuel energy boom.

I don't want to be partisan here. But please, tell me how you get out of a business recession by raising business taxes and regulations?

It may be coming, but so far Clinton has no corporate-tax reform plan. Even Barack Obama would have taken the business tax rate down to 28 percent. But Clinton has nothing.

And she has forgotten the economic lesson of the greatest Democratic politician of the last 50 years, John F. Kennedy.

JFK inherited three recessions from the Dwight D. Eisenhower years. And he wound up slashing tax rates across the board, for upper, middle and lower incomes as well as corporate investment. That's Kennedy the Democrat.

And when Republican Ronald Reagan faced stagflation in the 1980s, he went back in time and borrowed JFK's supply-side tax-cut program. And it worked for 20 years, throwing off 4-to-5 percent economies.

As a free-market guy, I love competition. That includes political competition. And what we need to get this economy out of its rut is a little tax-and-regulatory-cut competition between the two political parties.

The Democrats may be too hopelessly left to compete on this front. Today's liberals ignore the economic lessons of the JFK presidency. But Republicans, along with Trump, have studied the JFK-Reagan supply-side solution to boost economic growth. Alas, it's a one-sided competition.

As we come to the election homestretch, the issue is not going to be one month's jobs report, one quarter's gross domestic product number or one rate hike from the Fed. The No. 1 factor in this presidential campaign is who has the vision and strategy to lift up the wage-earning middle class, move America back onto the path to prosperity and get this country in a good and optimistic mood once again.

don't agree with Trump on everything. But his tax cuts and regulatory rollbacks will boost jobs, wages and the economy. He has the right economic message. And if he hammers away, day in and day out, repeating the basics of this message, he will win.

As Ronald Reagan taught us, repetition is the key to messaging.

Tax Cuts, King Dollar and Growth: From JFK to Reagan to Trump

September 17, 2016

Fifty-four years ago, at The Economic Club of New York, President John F. Kennedy unveiled a dramatic tax cut plan to revive the long-stagnant U.S. economy. He proposed lowering marginal tax rates for all taxpayers and reducing the corporate tax. He advised lowering the top tax rate from 91 to 65 percent, and closing tax loopholes. Five times during the speech he used the word "incentive."

In perhaps the most famous line from that path-forging speech, he said, "In short, it is a paradoxical truth that tax rates are too high today and tax revenues too low, and the soundest way to raise revenues in the long run is to cut rates now."

Kennedy had already in 1962 lowered investment taxes on business. And after his tragic assassination, in early 1964, his broader tax proposals were passed into law. And they worked. The U.S. economy grew by roughly 5 percent yearly for nearly eight years.

Almost 20 years later, President Ronald Reagan launched a 30 percent tax rate reduction to save the economy from the high-unemployment, high-inflation 1970s. Reagan acknowledged many times that he was following in Kennedy's footsteps. Under Reagan, also known as the Gipper, tax rates were slashed from 70 percent to 28 percent, corporate taxes were cut, and numerous loopholes were closed. And the American economy grew mostly between 4 and 5 percent annually for over 25 years.

Both Kennedy and Reagan followed a simple growth model that I call "tax cuts and King Dollar." Both men also reached across the aisle to garner bipartisan support for their plans.

This past week, Donald Trump went a long way toward joining their ranks. Speaking before The Economic Club of New York, he delivered a positive, optimistic message of growth that falls squarely inside the JFK-Reagan model.

"My economic plan," he said, "rejects the cynicism that our labor force will keep declining, that our jobs will keep leaving and that our economy will never grow as it did once before." Optimism.

He established a goal of 4 percent economic growth, which would double the stagnant rate of the past 15 years. The centerpiece of his plan is a reduction in business tax rates for large and small firms, to 15 percent from the current uncompetitive 35 percent. He offered immediate expensing for new investment, and a 10 percent repatriation rate to incentivize American firms overseas to bring $2.5 trillion home.

High business taxes are the biggest obstacle to a return to rapid economic growth. Abundant research has shown that the best way to raise wages and create jobs is to slash business taxes. Within five years a business tax cut will pay for itself, and then some.

Importantly, Trump plans to reduce individual tax rates to three brackets of 12, 25 and 33 percent. He would cap deductions for the wealthy and close special-interest loopholes. Middle-income wage earners will be the biggest beneficiaries of these reforms.

To cap it off, he will roll back out-of-control regulations, unleash American energy and abolish the Obamacare failure.

Following the successes of the JFK and Reagan tax reforms, Trump's strategy is likely to generate 4 to 5 percent growth over time. A rising tide will lift all boats.

The contrast between the presidential contenders could not be starker. Hillary Clinton would raise taxes on so-called rich people, corporations, capital gains, financial transactions and inheritance. Has there ever been an example of America taxing its way into prosperity? Never.

Trump has an economic recovery-and-prosperity plan. Clinton has an austerity-recession plan. Historically, in presidential elections, the optimistic growth plan nearly always wins.

That said, Trump's view of monetary policy, especially surrounding the dollar, needs to be resolved. During his speech, he charged that the Fed is "totally controlled politically." Elsewhere, he has stated that Fed Chair Janet Yellen is keeping interest rates ultralow in a political effort to boost Democratic fortunes. I disagree.

Yellen doesn't control the Fed monolithically. And the real debate about interest rates is going on inside the Fed.

True enough, the Fed needs radical reforms. In particular, it needs to replace its failed forecasting models and be rid of the academics who overwhelm the Fed system. But as New York Sun editor Seth Lipsky has taught us, the best way to depoliticize the Fed is to develop a standard of value, to make the dollar strong, reliable and stable. In other words, it's to develop a monetary rule.

JFK and Reagan's growth model included tax cuts and a steady dollar. Trump has taken a gigantic step toward restoring prosperity with his tax-cut-centered fiscal policy. Hopefully he will soon turn to a sound-dollar policy to bolster the growth impact of lower tax rates and regulations.

And hopefully he will then pound away on all this on the campaign trail.

Hillary's Red Army March of Tax-Hike Destruction

October 1, 2016

You've got to hand it to Team Hillary Clinton. Its message discipline is awesome — at least in terms of taxes. It reminds me of the orderly march of the Chinese Red Army on the way to battle.

Here's the latest message: The George W. Bush tax cuts were responsible for the financial meltdown and recession of 2008-09. That's a new low for Hillarynomics.

In this week's debate, Clinton said: "Trickle-down it did not work. It got us into the mess we were in in 2008 and 2009. Slashing taxes on the wealthy hasn't worked."

OK. So in 2003, President Bush got a modest reduction in the top income tax rate and bigger reductions in the tax rates on capital gains and dividends. And this caused the financial crisis? How it did is virtually unknowable.

My pal, American Enterprise Institute scholar Jim Pethokoukis, who's no Trump supporter, put it like this: "Wouldn't the George W. Bush tax cuts — most of which President Obama extended — have stimulated demand and/or improved supply-side incentives to work, save and invest?"

Pethokoukis cited an AEI study on inequality that found "strong evidence linking credit booms to banking crises, but no evidence that rising income concentration was a significant determinant of credit booms." He also pointed out that the Financial Crisis Inquiry Commission report blamed banks, regulators, government agencies and credit raters for the recession.

I would add to this list of culprits a boom-and-bust Federal Reserve policy, where interest rates were held too low for too long. And let's add federal housing mandates that virtually eliminated income and job qualifications for loans, as well as highly overleveraged bank mortgage loans and derivatives.

But not the Bush tax cuts.

Back to Hillary's Red Army. In recent debates with pro-Clinton economists, several of whom are good friends, I heard the same accusations — Bush and his so-called tax cuts for the rich are to blame.

I challenged one of these Clinton supporters to find me an example where across-the-board tax increases generated economic growth. Have we ever taxed our way into prosperity? Never. This particular Clinton defender acknowledged that across-the-board tax hikes would put a stop to prosperity. But he argued that that's not her plan.

Let me pull out my list of Clinton tax hikes: a $350 billion income tax increase in the form of a 28-percent cap on itemized deductions (without lowering personal tax rates); a more-than $400 billion "fairness" tax hike in the form of a 4 percent "surcharge" on high-end earners; and the "Buffet rule," which would establish a 30-percent minimum tax on earners with adjusted gross incomes over $1 million.

Clinton also proposes increasing the estate tax rate to a range of 45 to 65 percent and reducing the exemption to $3.5 million.

Remember, estate taxes are already hit once by the income tax, and again by the capital-gains tax. Here, Clinton would end the stepped-up capital gains tax basis and instead value the gain all the way back to the initial transaction.

One of my favorite economists, Scott Grannis, calls this legalized theft.

Clinton would also raise the capital gains tax to over 40 percent, unless gains are held for more than six years; cap various business deductions (without lowering the corporate rate); and install some sort of exit tax for corporate earnings overseas (which are overseas to avoid the high corporate rates she will not reduce).

Then, there's her proposed tax on stock trading, her attraction to a payroll tax hike, her openness to a carbon tax, and her endorsement of a steep soda tax and a 25 percent national gun tax.

If this list does not constitute across-the-board tax hikes, I don't know what would.

Now, contrast this with Trump's plan to reduce tax rates for individuals and large and small businesses (while abolishing the death tax).

His new 15 percent corporate tax-rate plan would unleash overseas-profits repatriation and a huge surge in corporate investment. By itself, the business tax reform could grow the economy by 4 percent.

But Trump has to be more persuasive. He could highlight how middle-income wage earners benefit most from lower business taxes. He could emphasize his tax cut on small mom-and-pop businesses. He could explain that lower individual tax rates boost what President Ronald Reagan called "take-home pay" — more money in your pocket. He could stress how lower business taxes lead to a large increase in incentives that boost investment, productivity, risk-taking, new business formation and worker wages.

The biggest issue in this campaign is the economy/wages/jobs. Trump must hammer home how his plan to boost all three contrasts drastically with Hillary's Red Army march of tax-hike destruction.

He has a prosperity plan. She has a recession plan.

Americans will always vote for prosperity. But the case has to be made.

Finding Strength in Melania Trump

October 20, 2016

When the now-infamous Donald Trump-Billy Bush audio feed was released, my confidence in Trump all but evaporated. The conversation about kissing, groping and fondling women was worse than so-called locker room talk. It was vile, vulgar and inexcusable for a grown man.

But it didn't end with the audio tape. After that came a barrage of sexual assault allegations from various women against Trump that drowned out any talk of substantive issues. No wonder his polls slid. He was a stock looking for a bottom.

During the second debate, just days after the audio tape release, he did apologize, and he did get to some key issues. I thought his stock might be finding a bottom.

But then he re-hit the campaign trail with bizarre statements about being the victim of a Mexican billionaire, major media outlets and rigged elections. His stock continued to slide.

In the meantime, a boatload of Hillary Clinton emails leaked out. Of course, we learned of unscrupulous deals, official favors for cash and how one of her former undersecretaries at the State Department tried to make a deal with the FBI to protect her.

Granted, sex sells better than emails. But both of these presidential candidates are in a race to the bottom for the worst untrustworthy rating in political history. It would seem the public has come to believe, rightly or wrongly, that Trump is a skirt-chaser and Clinton is incapable of telling the truth.

For Clinton I don't see redemption. She is a corrupt political operative of the worst kind. But for Trump I may see a way back. And his wife, Melania Trump, is a big reason why.

She gave some remarkable cable interviews this week, and she has me looking at the awful last two weeks in a somewhat different light.

Trump told CNN that her husband's words on the audio tape were not acceptable. In even stronger language, she told Fox News, "Those words, they were offensive to me, and they were inappropriate. And he apologized to me. And I expect — I accept his apology. And we are moving on."

I've only met Melania once, a few months ago at a funeral. For some reason, she recognized me. She came up, shook my hand and, if I recall correctly, thanked me for supporting her husband's tax-cutting economic plan.

And then she turned her head and in a strong voice said to Donald, who was a few bodies away, "Look who's here. Say hello."

I was surprised and impressed by her political skills. She also had a certain strength and toughness that reminded me she's a successful businesswoman.

When she told cable reporters that she accepted her husband's apology, I think she meant it.

We really hadn't heard from Melania Trump since these semi-scandals hit. She never showed up at that typical news conference — the wife dutifully staring up at that guilty-as-sin politician, playing the fawning bride beside the man who proceeds to lie through his teeth to the media.

When she repeated, "This is not the man that I know," it reminded me that he's not the man *I* know. In meetings in his office or on his plane, he was always a serious, accessible, engaged businessman-turned-politician, wading through important policy issues as he learned his craft.

True enough, Donald Trump has said some indefensible things this campaign. Many of us who have supported him have said so, and we will criticize him again if it comes to that.

But then again, how is it that all these women spontaneously come out of the woodwork with unverified stories about Trump? Again, I like how Melania Trump handled it: with great civility under pressure, instead of viciously attacking these women, as Clinton once did to her husband's accusers. Trump simply said, "All the allegations should be handled in a court of law."

She correctly makes one think that this phalanx of accusations is planned and organized. If not, why hasn't one accuser filed charges?

And she had one more thing to say — some advice for her husband: Get back to the issues.

Indeed, Donald Trump, if he is to regain his chance, must pivot back to economic growth, jobs, wages, Obamacare repeal, border security and destroying ISIS. Women, by the way, are just as worried about these issues as men.

It is doubtful that all this will be put to rest at Wednesday's debate. But Trump has one last opportunity to apologize to the nation, just as he apologized to his wife. And then he can tell us how his plan to get America right again is far better than Clinton's.

I want to thank Melania for starting me on the path of restored confidence in Donald Trump.

Just the Facts, Ma'am

October 29, 2016

We knew there could be a big October surprise before this bizarre and unpopular election finally came to an end. But who knew it would come from emails found on a device used by former Rep. Anthony Weiner, which was confiscated by the FBI after he sexted an underage woman — an act that cost him his job, his income and his marriage?

As I pondered this on Friday afternoon, I had a faint recollection of Winston Churchill describing a tough loss in an MP election. Hat tip to Susan Varga, who located this Churchill gem: "In a twinkling of an eye, I found myself without an office, without a seat, without a party, and without an appendix." Churchill had his appendix taken out during that election, which took place in 1922.

So let's see here. Anthony Weiner lost his office and his seat. And while I don't know about his appendix, he *did* lose his marriage for referring to matters below the waist.

And Huma Abedin, Hillary Clinton's aide and Weiner's soon to be ex-wife, may well lose her seat and her office, although I couldn't find any information about her appendix, despite a long Google search.

On the other hand, the FBI's bombshell that it is reopening the investigation into Hillary Clinton's private email server may well cause the Democratic presidential candidate to lose her office, her seat and her party. As to the condition of her appendix, we'll just have to guess, since no one knows the state of her deteriorating health.

And then we have FBI director James Comey, who may well be on his way to losing his office, his seat and his reputation. (I have no information on the status of his appendix.)

And how bizarrely ironic is it that Comey — who lost considerable credibility a couple of months ago for building an iron-clad case against Clinton only to let her off the hook — is now reopening her case based not on Russian espionage or Julian Assange's WikiLeaks, but on Anthony Weiner's electronic sex life?

This will not bring honor and glory to J. Edgar Hoover's venerable crime-fighting organization. Comey's announcement, by the way, follows hot on the heels of the revelation that Clinton pal and Virginia governor Terry McAuliffe channeled near $500,000 into the failed state senate campaign of Jill McCabe, who is the wife of FBI deputy director Andrew McCabe, who helped oversee the agency's investigation into Clinton's private email server. And let it be known that Hillary Clinton helped raise $1 million for McAuliffe's PAC.

Did any of these connections have anything to do with Clinton's getting off scot free from a criminal indictment? Nah.

But wait, could it be that Donald Trump's accusation that the system is rigged is correct after all?

Now, from Churchill to Jack Webb. Remember him? He played LAPD Detective Sergeant Joe Friday on the great Dragnet series. He opened the show with, "This is the city: Los Angeles, California. I work here. I'm a cop."

But the straight shooting Detective Friday may be better known for this deadpan phrase: "Just the facts, ma'am." Those are words that may go to the very heart of this presidential election.

No matter what James Comey unveils in the days ahead, if anything, virtually no one in this country believes Hillary Clinton will ever divulge "just the facts."

That's what the polls say, and for her they're getting worse. And that's exactly what the FBI bombshell has reminded the voting public. Clinton, Inc., is dishonest, above the law, on the take.

New WikiLeaks-provided emails from Clinton aide Doug Band reveal the true nature of the Clinton cash operation: No matter what the stated humanitarian goals of the Clinton Foundation, every fiber and sinew of the organization is wrapped in self-dealing, self-enrichment, fraud and corruption.

This is how the Clintons got rich. They traded cash for State Department visits and cash for government favors. And let's not forget those $450,000 speeches by Bill Clinton and those $250,000 speeches by Hillary herself.

And she can't even tell the truth about that, as leaked emails show that she said one thing to Wall Street and quite another to the public.

The election is a week and a half away, and the atmosphere has changed significantly. In the last several days, at long last, Donald Trump has been talking issues on the campaign trail. Issues like the economy, tax cuts, the need to repeal and rewrite Obamacare, and even African American inner-city problems. During this period, Hillary Clinton was deluged with email leaks and blindsided by the FBI.

Issues beat email leaks. Polls are rapidly narrowing. Suddenly, the potential for a GOP three-house electoral sweep is growing larger.

If Trump Wins, Buy the Dip.
If Clinton Wins, Sell the Rally

November 8, 2016

The wisdom on Wall Street is that Hillary Clinton is the safe choice. She's the certainty candidate to Donald Trump's uncertainty. So when Jim Comey announced the reopening of the FBI's Clinton investigation, stocks fell for nine days. And after he pulled back over the weekend, stocks rallied by over 300 points.

Is the market correct in viewing Clinton as the safe and certain choice? I don't believe so.

I'm not going to predict tonight's outcome, though I think it will be close. But I offer this advice: If Trump wins and stocks fall, buy the Trump dip. And if Clinton wins and stock rise, sell the Clinton rally.

By the way, Strategas investment ace Dan Clifton points out that when stocks fall in the months before a presidential election, it usually means the incumbent will lose. And Clinton is the incumbent — Obama 3.0. Investment pundits beware.

But the idea that Clinton is the "safe hands" candidate is plain wrong. If she wins, investigations will swirl around the Clinton Foundation's pay-to-play shenanigans. In this way, she has become the unsafe hand — the "high-risk candidate," as Wall Street Journal columnist Holman Jenkins puts it.

But what make her especially unsafe are her economic policies, which would damage growth, productivity, investment, wages and jobs.

Clinton proposes across-the-board tax hikes on corporations, successful earners, health care, capital gains and financial transactions. She would tax and spend her way to a nationalized, single-payer health system — a sure failure. She would end fossil fuels altogether. And rather than let market forces dictate America's energy portfolio, she'd return to Solyndra-like energy subsidies.

That would not be safe for the economy or stocks.

Essentially, her vision is to withdraw resources from the private free enterprise economy — robbing businesses and workers of crucial incentives to perform — and use these resources for another vast expansion of government power. She envisions a larger regulator state, even after the massive Obama regulations clogged the wheels of commerce.

What's more, she has been a weak candidate. She had trouble putting away Bernie Sanders and is now in the fight of her life against Trump. Translation: Elizabeth Warren and Bernie Sanders are the new ideological architects of a far-left Democratic Party that has completely written out of its history the great JFK tax reforms, which spurred a massive boom in the 1960s.

Now, Trump is a highly imperfect candidate. We all know that. But — and this is a big but — warts and all, Trump is an outsider who would work hard to drain the Washington, D.C., swamp of corruption, crony capitalism and corporate welfare. And only an outsider stands a chance of fixing this mess.

What's more, Trump is the growth candidate. His across-the-board tax rate reductions for individuals and businesses would boost the economy. His tax cuts for large and small businesses would re-incentivize startups and investment, from which productivity and real wages spring.

We have had a dismal 16 years of less than 2 percent growth, virtually no real wage hikes and stagnant family incomes — or what Ronald Reagan called take-home pay. Trump's economic plan would do for families what Democrats and Republicans have been unable to do in the past decade and a half.

n addition, Trump's repatriation incentives would bring home trillions of dollars. And his policies for low tax rates and immediate expensing of new investment would keep American businesses at home and win the race for global capital.

Tax reform most likely would be the first policy action in a Trump administration. A close second would be a thorough repealing and rewriting of Obamacare, restoring a freer market with true consumer choice and competition among providers.

Trump also would roll back the massive Obama regulatory overkill. He would take all the handcuffs off U.S. energy production, push for school choice, protect the southern border and send criminal undocumented immigrants back home for good.

The biggest flaw in the Trump economic plan is the tilt toward protectionism. I have parted company with him on this. The question here is whether his campaign bark will turn out to be bigger than his government policy bite if he wins.

Enforcing trade deals is spot on. Acting in the interest of American workers is correct. But large-scale tariffs are a terrible idea. My hunch is that Trump would promote better trade deals while minimizing tariffs. Ronald Reagan, Bill Clinton, George W. Bush and Barack Obama all used temporary targeted tariffs on specific industries. Let's hope Trump would go no further than that.

And as Trump has occasionally said, there are great benefits to trade. Let's hope he holds that thought.

I believe that Trump has a prosperity plan. I believe that Clinton has a recession plan. And you need an outsider to shake up Washington.

On Monday, I cast an absentee ballot for Donald Trump.

Why Not 100-Year U.S. Treasury Bonds?

December 15, 2016

If President-elect Donald Trump's economic growth plan — slashing business and personal marginal tax rates, and rolling back costly business regulations — is achieved next year, the economy could break out with 4 to 5 percent growth. And that means much higher interest rates.

This rate rise will be growth-induced — a good thing. Higher real capital returns will drive up real interest rates. And inflation will likely remain minimal, around 2 percent, with more money chasing even more goods alongside a reliably stable dollar exchange rate.

We're already seeing some of this with the big post-election Trump stock rally occurring alongside a largely real-interest-rate increase in bonds.

However, looking ahead, 4 percent real growth plus 2 percent inflation could imply 6 percent bond yields in the coming years. That's a big jump from the 2 percent average of most of the past 10 years.

And what that says is, the time to act is now.

The average duration of marketable Treasury bonds held by the public has been five years for quite some time. Almost incredibly, Treasury Department debt managers have not substantially lengthened the duration of bonds to take advantage of generationally low interest rates. It's hard to figure.

Treasuries held in public hands have moved up from 32 percent of gross domestic product back in 2008 to nearly 77 percent today. Interest expense for the 2016 fiscal year is nearly $250 billion. So if

Treasury debt managers had significantly lengthened their bond maturities, they would have saved taxpayers a bundle.

Now, with new economic growth policies poised to drive up average Treasury rates to, perhaps, 6 percent, the Treasury folks better get moving fast to capture today's historically low yields. Up till now they've been sleeping at the switch.

The key point is to start issuing longer bond maturities — much longer. If possible, the U.S. should experiment with 50-year debt issuance, and maybe as long as a 100-year issuance.

And this better happen fast.

According to economist Conrad Dequadros, other countries have been smarter than us. Ireland and Belgium issued 100-year debt. Austria issued 70-year debt. Italy, France and Spain issued 50-year debt. Japan pushed out a 40-year maturity, and there are rumors that it's considering 50 years.

And Mexico, incredibly enough, has done three 100-year issues since 2010. The sizes were small, and the bonds were sold in foreign currencies. But it can be done.

Britain is probably the best benchmark. HM Treasury has issued 40- to 50-year bonds seven times. The latest auction occurred in Oct. 2015, with the issuance of 50-year debt with a coupon of 2.5 percent.

Dequadros says the Congressional Budget Office estimates that interest costs over the next 10 years will total $4.8 trillion, and the debt will rise from the current $14 trillion to $23.1 trillion by 2026. Additionally, it expects the 10-year Treasury rate to average 3.3 percent and the rate on all debt to average 2.6 percent.

Now, with some very rough back-of-the-envelope calculations, under Trump's growth program, suppose 10-year Treasury rates rise to average 5 percent over the next 10 years, rather than the CBO's 3.3 percent guess. The average interest rate for all debt would increase to 4 percent over that period, rather than CBO's estimated 2.6 percent. The total interest rate expense would be around $7 trillion, rather than the CBO's $5 trillion baseline.

However, if the U.S. issued 50-year debt with the same rate as Britain's 2.5 percent, by front-loading some longer-term issuance to hold the average interest rate to 3.5 percent, there would be a $1 trillion savings on budget-interest expense over the 10-year horizon.

That's not chump change.

Skeptics will ask who would buy 50-year U.S. paper. It's a good question. But remember, insurance companies and pension funds need long-dated liabilities to match long-duration assets. And foreign institutions might also be interested in ultralong U.S. Treasuries, provided the U.S. dollar is reliably stable.

This is entirely new ground for U.S. debt management. But since a lot of foreign countries have successfully sold 50-year paper, we know it can be done.

And for the U.S. it must be done.

If we sell out a bunch of 50-year offerings, why not try a 100-year paper? The budget savings would be incalculable. And under new policies, if the U.S. returns to its long-term annual growth trend of 3.5 percent, which prevailed in the prior century, America's debt-to-GDP ratio could plunge to 30 or 40 percent, instead of skyrocketing to 150 percent or more.

Stronger growth and much longer bond-maturity issuance will snatch fiscal victory from the jaws of defeat.

The Trump Transition Is Transcendent, but the Economy Needs Attention Now

December 24, 2016

President-elect Donald Trump's transition continues to go smoothly. Actually, better than smoothly — confidently. More than confidently — transcendently.

And to top it all off, the Dow is up 9 percent since the election, while economic-sensitive small caps have jumped nearly 16 percent. These are signs of Trump confidence.

Hard-nosed investment manager Ray Dalio, founder of Bridgewater Associates and a nonpolitical guy, expects the Trump years to be as transformational as the years of President Ronald Reagan and Prime Minister Margaret Thatcher. He says the Trump era could "ignite animal spirits" and "shift the environment from one that makes profit makers villains with limited power to one that makes them heroes with significant power."

That's as good a summary as I have found.

Since the election, I have argued that the Barack Obama/Hillary Clinton war against business will come to an end and that America will once again reward success, not punish it. And while the left has demonized Trump's Cabinet appointees as a terrible group of successful business people, free-market capitalists such as myself regard this group as very good indeed.

Why shouldn't the president surround himself with successful people? Wealthy folks have no need to steal or engage in corruption. Their business success demonstrates that they know how to achieve goals and convince skeptics that good deals can be made to the benefit of both sides. Isn't this just what America needs?

And most of these folks aren't political. They won't be afraid to reach across the aisle for bipartisan solutions. And that includes Trump himself. For many years, he was a Democrat — just like Reagan, just like me.

In our new book, "JFK and the Reagan Revolution," Brian Domitrovic and I explain how the two great pro-growth tax-cutting presidents — John F. Kennedy, the Democrat, and Ronald Reagan, the Republican — used civility and respect to communicate key ideas in a bipartisan effort that yielded terrific results for American prosperity.

So far, this has been the Trump way. Not only has he conducted himself with great civility — beginning with his Oval Office meeting with President Obama — but he has also sought an inclusive approach wherever possible, irrespective of party.

Yet with less than a month until the inauguration, it is crucial that Trump embark on immediate bipartisan efforts to strengthen the economy. It was the number-one election-year issue. And despite strong post-election increases in business and consumer confidence — along with the stock rally — the economy is weakening yet again.

Measured year-to-year, real gross domestic product is rising only 1.7 percent. Business fixed investment, or BFI, continues to decline. Productivity is flat. Consumer spending has barely risen in the last two months, while both auto production and sales are slumping. Nonfinancial domestic profits have declined year to year for the last six quarters.

Of all these factors, the slump in business fixed investment is the most harmful. If you go back in history across the four long post-war recoveries of the '60s, '80s and '90s, BFI averaged nearly 7 percent. In the Obama recovery, BFI was only 4 percent. Over the past two years, it has been flat.

Using a back-of-the-envelope rule of thumb, if the investment performance of Presidents Kennedy, Reagan and Clinton were in place now, our economy would be growing at 3 percent rather than 2 percent — a big difference.

That's why pro-growth tax reform is so important. It is reported that Trump will immediately move to overturn costly Obama regulations, especially on small business. This is good. It will add to growth.

But the big decision will be whether to repeal and rewrite Obamacare or enact tax reform as the first order of legislative business.

Replacing Obamacare is hugely important, both to improve our health care system and remove the economic drag of its taxing, spending and regulating. But business tax reform — with low marginal corporate rates for large and small companies, easy repatriation and immediate expensing for new investment — will have an enormously positive impact on the weakest part of our economy, namely business investment.

That's where we'll see 3 or 4 percent growth, higher productivity, more and better-paying jobs and fatter family pocketbooks.

If there were a way to combine a two-year budget resolution with reconciliation instructions (51 Senate votes) to reform health care and taxes in one full sweep, that would be ideal. However, if tax reform (be it business or individual) comes second and the start dates are postponed until 2018, then businesses and consumers will postpone economic activity. That could make 2017 a much weaker economic story than confidence surveys and the recent stock market suggest.

There's a great transition going on, but the economy needs immediate attention. Tax reform is the key.

'We Must Think Big and Dream Even Bigger'

January 25, 2017

In all the media back and forth over President Donald Trump's inaugural speech, most have missed a central point: His address was infused with a wonderful sense of optimism.

As an old Ronald Reagan guy, I have learned through the years that optimism equals true leadership. And yes, true leadership cannot be achieved without optimism.

Toward the end of his speech, Trump said, "We must think big and dream even bigger." To understand Trump and his message on Inauguration Day is to appreciate the importance of that sentence.

He then added: "The time for empty talk is over. Now arrives the hour of action. Do not let anyone tell you it cannot be done. No challenge can match the heart and fight and spirit of America. We will not fail. Our country will thrive and prosper again."

All the media's talk about the so-called dark nature of the speech completely obscured these crucial lines.

I don't know about you, folks, but I am tired of all this talk of permanent American decline, secular stagnation, a new normal that dooms us to slow growth, falling living standards, weak middle-class wages and all the rest.

You hear it enough that you could almost come to believe it.

Yes, in recent years, the country has fallen into a pessimistic funk. But this is not the America I know. And far more important, it's not the America President Trump wants.

Trump was a change candidate who blasted away at the establishment's failures at the expense of ordinary Main Street folk. And he successfully ran with the simple idea that things can be fixed. And he brought that optimism to his inaugural address.

As he said: "Now arrives the hour of action. Do not let anyone tell you it cannot be done."

Decades ago, when Reagan was elected president, the intellectual consensus was that high inflation, high unemployment and American decline could not be changed. The idea was that the country was ungovernable.

But Reagan put an end to that. He did it with a clear set of easy-to-understand policies to fix the economy and restore American leadership abroad. And he guided that plan into place with his quintessential optimism.

Trump and Reagan are very different people. And Trump's governing style will be nothing like Reagan's. But the underlying principle of optimism is the same.

"Finally, we must think big and dream even bigger," he said. How quintessentially American is that? Can we return to being the proverbial City Upon a Hill? Yes, we can.

For these reasons I believe President Trump has the potential to be a transformational figure. And he is moving fast. His actions and energy in just the first couple of days have been remarkable.

Everywhere he repeats the theme of economic growth with lower taxes and fewer burdensome regulations. The war on business is over. We will reward success, not punish it.

He talks bilateral trade deals that can be enforced. He is freezing federal hiring, proposing to cut government spending $10.5 trillion over 10 years, doing away with Obamacare mandates, getting the Keystone XL and Dakota Access pipelines in place, welcoming a constant flow of visitors from businesses and unions and taking calls from foreign heads of state.

He has set up a meeting with British Prime Minister Theresa May, moving a U.S.-Britain free-trade agreement from the back of the queue to the front.

He is making it clear that he will seek border security, replace catch-and-release with catch-and-deport, institute skills-based legal immigration (rather than family-based), deport criminal illegals and end sanctuary cities.

Following up on his inaugural pledge to eradicate the Islamic State group — to "unite the civilized world against radical Islamic terrorism, which we will eradicate completely from the face of the Earth," as he said — he is calling for a military strategy memo from the joint chiefs and backing an allied coalition of ground forces to take the IS stronghold in Raqqa, Syria.

There will be no more containment of IS, but rather the eradication of IS. We have wanted to hear this for years. Trump said it, and he means it.

Finally, conservative journalists are recognized at the beginning of press conferences; Cabinet nominees are getting through confirmation; and Republicans on the Hill are finding they can work with the new president.

In all this — from strength at home to strength abroad — Trump is moving at warp speed. And he is keeping to his inaugural pledge that "Every decision on trade, on taxes, on immigration, on foreign affairs will be made to benefit American workers and American families."

This is what he ran on. Thankfully, he is not about to change. And that's why he has the potential for greatness.

Right now, I truly wish folks would help him, not seek to harm him. Give him a chance.

We must think big and dream even bigger.

Tax and Regulatory Reform Will Mark the End of Obama's War on Business

February 14, 2017

On the very day President Donald Trump's incentive-based tax and regulatory policies are put in place, former President Barack Obama's war on business will have officially come to an end. No longer will American companies be punished by uncompetitive rates of taxation and unnecessary rules and regulations.

Business tax rates are coming down from roughly 40 percent to 15 or 20 percent, which is not only a boon for business but also a godsend for the middle class. Slashing business tax rates for both large and small businesses will generate significant new investment, jobs and growth, all of which will lead to higher wages.

And when people and businesses get to keep more of what they earn, more of what they invest and more of what they risk, they are incentivized to keep doing more of these activities.

In essence, that's the Trump economic plan. The president is saying, "We will reward success, not punish it." He's also saying, "The war against business is over."

And that means growth, growth, growth.

You want to lower the budget deficit? You want to lower the debt-to-growth domestic product ratio? Then grow the economy. Not by 1 or 2 percent, which is the lackluster growth rate that solidified during the Obama years, but by 3 or 4 percent.

That level of consistent economic growth will solve a lot of problems. Every 1 percentage point in GDP above the baseline, which is 2 percent today, cuts deficits by more than $3 trillion over 10 years.

A U.S. manufacturing boom and more companies staying and making things at home — those are great things. But I don't want the U.S. to be an export-led economy. I want us to once again be a market-driven economy. And if we reinvigorate market incentives with tax and regulatory reform, we will once again be king of the hill for economic growth.

Anemic growth is what the rest of the world does. And I don't want us to be the rest of the world. I don't want us to be semi-socialists. I don't want the United States to have a value-added tax, or VAT. I want us to be free market capitalists, and I want all the growth that comes with that.

And just imagine an incentive-driven free market capitalist economy in which tax dollars collected are put to good use, not squandered. I'm not opposed to government-spending restraint at all. I would like to get rid of the Department of Labor. The Department of Commerce can go, too. I would like to cut all the waste, fraud and abuse in Washington, D.C., that's possible.

Incentive-based tax policy plus "drain the swamp" is an excellent model for the future of America.

But one of the keys to President Trump's economic success will be strong and clear guidance, and I'm not completely sure the president is receiving such solid advice right now. Someone needs to explain to him the actual consequences of his fiscal plans. Cause-and-effect scenarios need to be mapped out, at least so there are no surprises down the road.

For instance, Trump is talking about lower trade gaps and a weaker dollar. Well, if his lower tax and regulatory policies go through and work as I believe they will, the reverse will occur. The dollar will strengthen, and trade gaps will widen. Somebody needs to sit with the president and say: "Think about this: Here are some charts that show what happened in the past when across-the-board tax cuts and regulatory reforms were put in place."

History shows that growth-driven trade deficits are merely the flip side of massive capital inflows from around the world. That's a good thing, not a bad one. Additionally, a strong and stable King

Dollar will generate investment confidence at home and abroad and hold down inflation — another good thing.

The first few weeks of the Trump administration have not been short of controversy. But they've also been filled with promise. The president is proving right out of the gate that he's both a man of his word and someone who gets things done.

But let me put my vote in for the primacy of tax and regulatory reform — in particular, a reduction of the corporate tax rate from 40 percent to 15 or 20 percent. This is the backbone of President Trump's growth policies. As such, business tax reform should come early, not late.

It would be best for it to come in the first reconciliation bill this spring. Otherwise, if it comes late this year or next year, the 2017 economy and stock markets will disappoint as people postpone activity until they are certain of the lower tax rates and the rules that will accompany them.

The end of Obama's war on business cannot come fast enough. Neither can renewed economic growth. Early tax reform is the key.

As Trump Unmuzzles the Economy, a Rosy Scenario Will Become Economic Reality

February 28, 2017

Virtually the whole world is beating up on the Trump administration for daring to predict that low marginal tax rates, regulatory rollbacks and the repeal of Obamacare will generate 3 to 3.5 percent economic growth in the years ahead.

In a CNBC interview last week, Treasury Secretary Steven Mnuchin held the line on this forecast. He also argued the need for dynamic budget scoring to capture the effects of faster growth. Good for him.

But what's so interesting about all the economic growth naysaying today is that former President Obama's first budget forecast roughly eight years ago was much rosier than President Trump's. And there was nary a peep of criticism from the mainstream media outlets and the consensus of economists.

Strategas Research Partners policy analyst Dan Clifton printed up a chart of the Obama plan that predicted real economic growth of roughly 3 percent in 2010, nearly 4 percent in 2011, over 4 percent in 2012 and nearly 4 percent in 2013.

But it turned out that actual growth ran below 2 percent during this period. Was there any howling about this result among the economic consensus? Of course not. It seems it has saved all its grumbling for the Trump forecast.

And what's really interesting is that the Obama policy didn't include a single economic growth incentive. Not one. Instead, there was a massive $850 billion so-called spending stimulus (Whatever became of those spending multipliers?), a bunch of public works programs that never got off the ground and, finally, Obamacare, which really was one giant tax increase.

Remember when Supreme Court Chief Justice John Roberts ruled that the health-care mandate was in fact a tax? But it wasn't just a tax. It was a tax hike. And added to that were a 3.8 percent investment tax hike, a proposed tax hike on so-called Cadillac insurance plans and yet another tax increase on medical equipment.

So eight years ago, tax-and-spend was perfectly OK. And the projection that it would produce a 4 percent growth rate perfectly satisfied the economic consensus.

Make sense? No, it does not.

So here's President Trump reaching back through history for a common-sense growth policy that worked in the 1960s, when President John F. Kennedy slashed marginal tax rates on individuals and corporations, and again in the 1980s, when President Ronald Reagan slashed tax rates across the board and sparked a two-decade boom of roughly 4 percent real annual growth.

But the economic consensus won't buy Trump's plan.

One after another, Trump critics argue that because we've had 2 percent growth over the past 10 years or so, we are doomed to continue that forever. This is nonsense.

Most of them point to the decline in productivity over the past 15 years. They say that unless productivity jumps to 2.5 percent or so, and unless labor-force participation rises, we can't possibly have 3 to 4 percent growth.

Stanford University economics professor John Taylor, who's also a research fellow at the Hoover Institution, is one of the nation's top academic economists. He released a chart on productivity growth that shows that productivity declines can be followed by productivity increases, which unfortunately can be followed again by productivity declines.

In his widely read blog, Economics One, Taylor wrote one post titled "Take Off the Muzzle and the Economy Will Roar." He notes that bad economic policy leads to slumping productivity, living standards, real wages and growth.

We can see "huge swings in productivity growth in recent years," he says. "These movements ... are closely related to shifts in economic policy, and economic theory indicates that the relationship is causal."

He concludes, "To turn the economy around we need to take the muzzle off, and that means regulatory reform, tax reform, budget reform, and monetary reform." Well, aren't those exactly the reforms that President Trump is promoting?

Get rid of the state-sponsored barriers to growth. Then watch how these common-sense incentive-minded policies turn a rosy scenario into economic reality.

Optimism Reigned in Trump's First Address to Congress

March 2, 2017

The mark of great presidents is optimism — visionary optimism and transformational optimism. During Tuesday night's remarkable speech before Congress, President Donald Trump was brimming with optimism from start to end. My guess is that his marvelous speech will imbue and inspire new optimism and confidence throughout the entire country.

The Dow Jones industrial average surged 300 points the day after the speech, and I'll bet the president's approval ratings jump over 20 points.

There are so many Trump cynics and critics who watched this event and hoped for a train wreck, a shock-value disaster. Whoops. It didn't happen. They completely misjudged Trump.

He wasn't angry. He didn't lash out. His voice was calm and modulated. And he was incredibly effective.

In fact, he was riveting. You couldn't take your eyes off him. You couldn't even take a bathroom break. You didn't want to miss a word.

President's Trump's speech was infused with civility, which is something we all hoped for as an alternative to the coarseness of American politics (and the rest of the culture, for that matter).

He made fact-based arguments on the economy, health care, education, immigration, national security and public safety. And he did so respectfully. He attempted to persuade, and it was wonderful to watch.

Time and again, he reached across the aisle to the Democrats. This was a unity speech, not a partisan one. The president asked for common ground and common good. He was saying, let's work together to solve all these problems that have troubled us for so many years.

I have no idea how the Democrats will respond. But poll after poll has shown that the country yearns for bipartisanship rather than the flame-throwing, name-calling political contentiousness that has governed Washington, D.C., and the campaign trail for so long.

All the Trump campaign themes were there. He intends to keep his promises. I thought he was especially convincing on merit-based immigration. And he set out the principles of health care reform, education choice and law and order everywhere, especially in the big inner cities where poverty has ruled alongside violence in a downward spiral that seems impossible to fix.

In recent days, the president has spoken to various business groups about 3 percent-plus economic growth, which would generate far more revenues and far fewer deficits than conventional pessimistic economists argue. During the speech before Congress, the president stuck to his guns on both economic growth and tax reform.

On foreign affairs, he pledged to stay with NATO, but he reminded everyone that his job is to protect the interests of the United States first and foremost.

On trade, his message was more ambiguous. Outright protectionism was muted, but the threat hangs in the air. The divisive border-adjustment tax looks to be part of a White House-Republican Party congressional deal, which is unfortunate. But let's wait on that to see the full story.

There's also the threat of a new GOP entitlement in the form of refundable tax credits. But let's wait on that as well, until the budget details are released.

Of course, there was the heartbreaking salute to Carryn Owens, the widow of U.S. Navy SEAL Chief William "Ryan" Owens. It was followed by long thunderous applause. It was an incredible and unforgettable moment.

And then, the president concluded: "We want peace, wherever peace can be found. ... Hopefully, the 250th year for America will see a world that is more peaceful, more just, and more free."

He pointed to Bell's telephone, Edison's telegraph and Remington's typewriter, suggesting that working together we can empower our aspirations and put aside our fears.

"But we can only get there together," he said. "We are one people with one destiny. We all bleed the same blood. We all salute the same great American flag. And we are all made by the same God."

That is optimism. That is leadership. And that is greatness. Both Trump's allies and doubters will now sleep better and with a little more hope than many of them will dare to admit.

Speeches like this can change history. Do not underestimate this president. Like tens of millions, I'm sure, I'm proud of him.

To Make the AHCA Better, the GOP Has to Practice Bipartisanship Within Itself

March 15, 2017

The good should never be the evil of the perfect. House Speaker Paul Ryan's health care bill is a very good first step. Massive repeal of Obamacare tax hikes will be great for the economy. Getting rid of the Affordable Care Act mandates will be great for health care. Private-sector competition and choice are always better than government-run anything. The Republican Party has to practice bipartisanship within itself.

All this health care reform stuff makes my head spin. And that's why I'm putting all my conclusions at the top of this piece.

I think the House and Senate GOP can make the Ryan blueprint even better. And I'm hopeful that the congressional leadership, along with President Trump's administration, will do just that.

But let's review a couple key points about the bill, the American Health Care Act, or AHCA. (There's no way to go through this whole deal.)

First, there's no point in obsessing over the Congressional Budget Office numbers. Its Obamacare enrollment predictions were so off the mark that there's no reason to believe its AHCA estimates will be any better. And we have so little experience, so little data and such massive reform that I don't think anybody could accurately model it. In this case, policies are the key, not forecasts. Americans are a lot smarter than the professors think.

But one thing that really astonishes me is that both the CBO and the Joint Committee on Taxation, or JCT, continue to stick to static estimates on tax changes. To wit: The biggest tax-hike repeal in the AHCA is the net investment income tax, which is primarily the capital gains tax. The CBO and JCT score it as a $158 billion loss over 10 years. Yet history nearly always teaches us that when the cap gains tax rate is cut, there's more investment, more risk-taking, more new business start-ups and more economic growth — and hence, higher revenues.

Ryan Ellis of Forbes was the first to point out the pro-growth tax-cutting advantages of the ACHA. They weren't perfect but were really good.

I count 13 tax cuts in the Ryan bill. And you could argue that these cuts will segue right into the Trump tax-reform proposals for business and individuals.

Stubbornly, I still believe that the business tax-reform package — nice and simple, with repatriation, lower rates and immediate expensing — should be grafted onto the health care reconciliation bill. Technically, this is possible. In fact, some of the new health care regulations, which are supposed to come later, could also be tacked onto the reconciliation package.

This might all come down to a new Senate parliamentarian, but so be it.

Next, health care expert Betsy McCaughey has been writing about the need to separate two groups — the healthy and the seriously ill. The sickest 5 percent of Americans consume 50 percent of the nation's health care. Addressing this, Ryan includes taxpayer-funded grants to states that establish new high-risk pools. But that may not be enough.

America is a generous nation. To help roughly 500,000 sick people in the individual market, the federal government should transparently subsidize this group, perhaps in the form of vouchers, or guarantee a national risk pool. The cost would be a third of Obamacare subsidies. The GOP should say this explicitly.

And this is the key: If you separate out the healthy from the ill, insurance premiums will plummet.

Ironically, with more choices and plunging premiums, millennials and other groups might choose to enter the private insurance exchange market and thereby increase enrollment into the AHCA. Think of it. Incentives matter.

Another point: The Ryan tax-credit subsidies look too generous to upper-end earners and insufficiently generous to lower-income earners. Avik Roy, president of the Foundation for Research on Equal Opportunity, finds that age-adjusted and means-tested refundable tax credits should focus on individuals earning $40,000 to $50,000 and families with children earning up to perhaps $70,000. These are the working-class folks who need help. A tax credit for someone earning $150,000 strikes me as way too high.

And for the people in poverty at the low end, smooth the benefit cliff as much as possible to avoid incentives for a poverty trap.

Elsewhere, Medicaid reform must be done very carefully. And the insurance company giveaway, which allows insurers to slap a 30 percent penalty on late enrollees, should be abolished.

Of course, there's a lot more inside the Ryan plan. But through all this complexity, we should not lose sight of the fact that however amended, the AHCA will abolish mandates, open the door to free-market choice and competition, provide universal access, generously protect the poor and the sick among us, and slash taxes, all of which give us a stronger health system and a faster growing economy.

So now the GOP has to practice bipartisanship within itself. Let's get to it.

Middle-Income Wage Earners Need a W — Cut Business Taxes First

April 1, 2017

After the breakdown of health care reform, both President Trump and the Republican Congress need a W — a win.

And not just any win but one that will play into the public demand for faster economic growth, better jobs and higher wages. Recent polls show the nexus of growth, jobs and tax cuts vastly outranks health care.

So, most important, middle-class wage earners need a W. We've had job creation, but it hasn't reached all sectors of the population. Consequently, the employment-to-population ratio remains historically low. So does real gross domestic product growth.

From 1950 to 2000, growth averaged 3.5 percent a year. During President Obama's recovery — and, frankly, going back to the year 2000 — growth has hovered at only 2 percent per year. Real wages have barely improved. New business startups have actually declined. And productivity has flattened.

The hole in the center of this tepid growth story is a lack of business investment. It's the missing ingredient. From 1950 to 2000, total business fixed investment averaged a strong 5.3 percent annual growth. But since 2000, that figure has dropped to only 1.7 percent.

For 50 years, the capital-labor ratio (K/L ratio) increased by an average 3 percent a year. The capital stock rose 4.3 percent per year. But since 2009, the K/L ratio has fallen by 0.2 percent per year, and the capital stock has grown by only 1.5 percent yearly. This is why productivity and wage gains have been minimal. And the root cause is the lack of business investment.

But the GOP can remedy this by providing new tax incentives (including a rollback of costly regulations) right now. Specifically, the new Republican priority should be business tax cuts first.

While health care reform simmers on the back burner, the president should go right to business tax reform. It can be nice and simple and easy to understand. There's virtually a bipartisan consensus for it. Separate it out from the broader and far more complex and controversial issues related to individual tax reform.

Yes, we desperately need personal-tax simplification. We also need lower tax rates across the board. We need to clamp down on loopholes and unnecessary crony-capitalist deductions to broaden the tax base. But that's a much more difficult and longer battle. Save it for next year.

There are hundreds of tax lawyers in Washington, D.C., who can separate out business income from personal income. That will allow legislation to reduce tax rates for the small S-corp companies, as well as limited liability partnerships and proprietorships.

So let's end the war on business. Let's reward success, rather than punish it. Congress need only go for a 10 percent repatriation rate, a 15 to 20 percent tax rate for large and small businesses, and immediate expensing for new investments.

And perhaps to draw in some Democrats, legislators can use part of the roughly $200 billion in repatriation revenues to provide an equity base for an infrastructure fund that is privately owned and run. No new Fannie Mae or Freddie Mac. No government directors. Keep it all in the private sector.

And forget the crazy border-adjustment tax, or BAT. It would badly damage consumers and the economy, when what we need is faster growth.

Meanwhile, don't obsess over various reconciliation rules. Reconciliation can be whatever you want it to be. The so-called Byrd Rule, which stipulates deficit neutrality over the long run, has been broken many times over the past 30 years.

And maybe this time the GOP will talk to the Senate parliamentarian. Or perhaps the president of the Senate — Vice President Pence can overrule the parliamentarian.

With lower business tax rates and more net business investment to grow the capital stock, the economy is capable of growing over 3 percent yearly. And that 1 percentage point increase from the 2 percent baseline would yield, according to the Congressional Budget Office, more than $3 trillion in deficit reduction over the next 10 years.

The misbegotten BAT, and its phony $1 trillion pay-for, can be buried in a deep gravesite inside a large crypt.

Perhaps the major selling point for business tax cuts is the fact that the biggest beneficiaries are middle-income wage earners, not so-called rich people and rich corporations.

Importantly, the best research on this has been done by Kevin Hassett of the American Enterprise Institute and in recent years supported by a number of papers. Ironically, Hassett is slated to be chairman of the president's Council of Economic Advisors, as soon as his vetting process is complete. No one makes the case better than Hassett that business tax cuts are a middle-class tax cut.

So, with the postponement of health care reform, we now have more than four months before the August recess to give the country the fuel injection it needs: a boost for wage earners, businesses and consumers, productivity and better jobs.

Put business tax cuts first. Right now.

Tactical Nuclear Option
Inside Reconciliation

April 11, 2017

"Drain the swamp." It was one of President Trump's most powerful messages on the way to victory. Shake up Washington, D.C. Break a few eggs to create a new omelet. Overturn the establishment.

Well, hats off to Senate Majority Leader Mitch McConnell for doing some swamp draining when he exercised the "nuclear option" to overturn the filibuster for a Supreme Court justice confirmation. McConnell busted an old 19th-century rule, which was never in the Constitution, and cleared the path for the confirmation of Judge Neil Gorsuch — who's as good a candidate as can be found. Good for McConnell.

But let's shift our swamp draining focus to fiscal policy. Back in 1974, in the aftermath of Watergate, it was established that House and Senate budget committees would come together to pass a bill with something called "reconciliation instructions." In this way, they would move a product through the committees that would only require 51 votes in the Senate to pass.

The process was allegedly designed to promote fiscal sanity, such as curbing the nation's appetite for debt. Well, that didn't work. Federal debt in public hands was about 23 percent of gross domestic product back in the mid-1970s. Today it's about 77 percent of national income. Not much discipline there.

But the key problem with reconciliation is the highly flawed economic model used to score tax bills. Namely, the Congressional

Budget Office, or CBO, and the Joint Committee on Taxation, or JCT, score tax relief as a revenue loser and tax increases as revenue gainers. Clearly, such modeling makes it very difficult to reduce marginal tax rates.

And in recent years, this static modeling has led to the notion that tax cuts need a "pay-for." If you don't cut the budget enough, you don't get your tax cut.

Almost weirdly, the scorekeepers are happy with tax hikes, allegedly to balance the budget. But tax hikes depress economic growth, which reduces GDP. And with a smaller income base, actual revenues decline simply because most everybody is worse off.

In truth, the best way to balance the budget is to reduce tax rates and provide new incentives for faster growth, which then expands the income base and throws off more revenues.

In our book "JFK and the Reagan Revolution," Brian Domitrovic and I quote Democrat John F. Kennedy in his 1962 speech to the Economic Club of New York. With high drama, JFK turned against the New Deal, saying: "It is a paradoxical truth that tax rates are too high today (91 percent top rate) and tax revenues too low, and the soundest way to raise revenues in the long run is to cut rates now. ... The reason is that only full employment can balance the budget, and tax reduction can pave the way to that employment."

Twenty years later, Republican Ronald Reagan duplicated the JFK tax cuts to liberate a stagflationary economy. Today, the JFK-Reagan approach would rescue a stagnant economy.

But the scorekeepers stand in the way. They're part of the swamp. They're telling President Trump you cannot lower tax rates without pay-fors.

So I'd say it's time for a "tactical nuclear option inside reconciliation," as playfully put by Wall Street Journal reporter Richard Rubin. Throw out the static models and replace them with dynamic scoring that recognizes the positive impact of lower tax-rate incentives on growth.

The CBO estimates real economic growth over the next 10 years will continue to stagnate at a 1.8 percent annual pace. However, looking at history, we know that growth will increase with more take-home pay and handsome rewards for business.

How about a 3 percent growth rate over the next 10 years? It's still below America's long-run average. But if you slash tax rates, particularly on large and small business, it is reasonable to assume more investment, new companies, profits, productivity, wages and job creation.

Get this: According to former Senate budget expert Mike Solon, an economy growing at 3.1 percent per year would generate $4.5 trillion more revenues than an economy growing at 1.8 percent. Now that's a pay-for.

Growth is the best pay-for.

Turns out, under the rules of reconciliation, dynamic growth estimates are perfectly legal. Don't even have to blow up a filibuster. And Dan Clifton of Strategas Research Partners points out that the Senate parliamentarian says it's fine to use dynamic estimates. Why has Congress been using static forecasts all these years? They're nothing more than a bizarre tradition.

So if Sen. Mike Enzi, chairman of the Senate Budget Committee, decides to use dynamic scoring, the Trump tax-cut proposals will sail through.

Reconciliation can be whatever you want it to be. It just takes a bit of bravery to buck tradition and drain the static-thinking economic swamp.

Give wage earners and the entire economy the rocket boost they so badly need.

Don't Bet Against Tax and Health Care Reform in 2017

May 20, 2017

If the smart money folks on Wall Street think a special counsel to oversee the Russian probes spells defeat for business tax cuts, they're leaning well over their skis.

The Dow Jones industrial average sold off over 300 points on Wednesday, but it may have come back to its senses with a 140-point gain on Friday. And while there's never 100 percent probability in forecasting political risk, it seems the likelihood of health care reform by the summer and tax reform by year's end (or early 2018) is quite high.

Paradoxically, special counsel Robert Mueller will provide cover for President Trump, as it will take him many months to complete his investigation. The leaks are going to dry up. By law, information on the probe must be protected. So, whatever the outcome, Trump will have months without the attack headlines in which to sell his tax-cut plan.

Meanwhile, amid all the controversies, the GOP Congress knows it could get whacked in next year's midterms if it doesn't govern — a big incentive.

And Trump still has the backing of his core base, which is at least 40 percent of the electorate. These disenchanted voters may not agree with everything he says. But they still strongly believe Trump is their best chance to drain the swamp — to overturn the Beltway elites, to deliver border security, to improve trade deals and to cut taxes and regulations to deliver the full-fledged deeply rooted sustainable prosperity we haven't seen in 20 years.

Warts and all, Trump and his polices is still their vote. (He needs to go out there and rally these folks.)

And all this talk of impeachment based on obstruction of justice is just Democratic political pap. George Washington University law professor Jonathan Turley, who is no partisan, calls it "an awfully thin soup." Former federal prosecutor and National Review contributor Andrew McCarthy says, "the basis for claiming at this point that President Trump obstructed justice is not there." Acting FBI director Andrew McCabe told Congress there's been no interference in the FBI's investigations and no request for additional funding.

And if Comey did write a memo about obstruction of justice, he is legally obligated to report it to the highest levels of the Justice Department. Failure to do so could invoke criminal charges.

Why did he wait until he was fired to have his leakers put this out?

Yet behind all this mess, House Speaker Paul Ryan keeps telling people that Congress can walk and chew gum at the same time. He's right.

Look, the House has already passed a replacement of Obamacare. And a Senate health care working group led by top Republican leaders, including Sens. Lamar Alexander and Ted Cruz, is making progress resolving key issues between moderates and conservatives. There's no reason why the American Health Care Act can't become law by the August recess.

And that opens the door for taxes.

House Ways and Means Committee chair Kevin Brady just began expert tax hearings. After the recess, Brady will likely convene a markup session.

Rep. Peter Roskam, who chairs the congressional tax policy subcommittee, said last week, "I'm of the view that 2017 is the year." He thinks tax reform is easier than replacing Obamacare.

So, following a markup, Ways and Means can report out a bill. And because prosperity is America's No. 1 issue, it will pass the floor relatively easily. And that will put pressure on the Senate to get moving.

It's likely that a tax cut working group will again convene to hash out important details. The border-adjusted tax, or BAT, will have to go. But the very core of the tax bill is a simple three steps: a deep corporate tax-rate cut, immediate expensing for new equipment of all kinds and the repatriation of offshore cash. This is the tonic that will restore capital formation, productivity, real wages and growth.

Both Senate and House leaders have to understand how flexible reconciliation is. It can be nearly anything you want it to be. The key player is Senate President Mike Pence, who can overrule the parliamentarian.

Congressional leaders should heed the words of Treasury Secretary Steven Mnuchin, who has become the administration's leading spokesperson for economic growth and lower tax rates. He told the Senate Banking Committee last week, "What I have said repeatedly is that any plan we put forward we believe should be paid for with economic growth."

He is estimating a 3 percent growth rate by 2021. I suspect it will arrive faster. And the difference between growth of less than 2 percent from the Congressional Budget Office and 3 percent growth is well over $3 trillion in additional revenue. It's the mother of all pay-fors.

And lowering marginal tax rates across the board, especially on large and small businesses, will foster the mother of all prosperities — the one for which middle-class Americans in all those red counties that voted for Trump have been yearning.

President Trump's Growth Budget

May 30, 2017

When Office of Management and Budget Director Mick Mulvaney unveiled President Trump's new budget, he used language that is so important — although we haven't heard it in so many years.

To paraphrase Mulvaney, the measure of budget success for the Trump administration is not how much federal assistance is given out but how many people leave government dependency and join the private labor force as full-fledged workers.

The last time I heard a talk like this was over 20 years ago when then-President Bill Clinton teamed with then-House Speaker Newt Gingrich to pass welfare reform. They argued that tighter eligibility, time limits, work search mandates and better training programs would move people from welfare to workfare.

Critics said, "Wait. No — tougher welfare requirements will throw millions onto the streets with no federal assistance." Turns out they were wrong. Millions moved into the labor force to work productively, grow the economy and provide themselves with new self-esteem and happiness.

The point on happiness is one of my favorites. I learned it from American Enterprise Institute President Arthur Brooks, who has done a number of quantitative surveys that clearly show how people who work for a living are far happier than those who depend on government assistance.

So, now, over 20 years later, Mulvaney is talking workfare over welfare. And, of course, the left-wing screaming has begun.

But something must be done. Almost eight years after the recession trough, government benefits for welfare, food stamps (Forty-four million people received food stamp benefits in 2016, compared with 14 million in December 2007), Medicaid and Social Security Disability Insurance are still exploding.

By tightening eligibility and putting back time limits and various work requirements, millions will return to the labor force, just as they did in the mid-1990s.

University of Chicago economics professor Casey Mulligan calls this the "redistribution recession." That is, the best of government intentions have actually backfired by reducing incentives to work and earn.

The expansion of food stamps, welfare, health insurance subsidies, unemployment assistance and disability assistance have led to unintended consequences and perverse after-tax incentives, such that it pays more to stay on assistance then to go to work. At the working-poor margin, taking a job may rob you of Obamacare subsidies, so it's better off not to work.

A couple of years ago, Mulligan estimated that the marginal tax rate — the extra taxes paid and subsidies forgone as the result of working — had increased from 40 percent to 48 percent in two years. Progressives hate this viewpoint. But Mulligan summed it up by saying: "Helping people is valuable but not free. The more you help low-income people, the more low-income people you'll have. The more you help unemployed people, the more unemployed people you'll have."

The left is also up in arms because Trump is "slashing" the budget. He's taking food out of the mouths of babies! Killing people for lack of health insurance! Throwing Granny in the wheelchair off the side of the cliff!

But here's a big-picture point: In most cases, the new budget merely slows the rate of spending growth.

Manhattan Institute economist Diana Furchtgott-Roth argues that what the media calls "cuts" are really increases. She's right. The so-called current services baseline goes up every year at 4, 5, 6 or 7 percent or more. So any reduction in the rate of increase is not a cut from last year's spending level.

The Trump budget proposes to raise government spending from $4 trillion today to $5.7 trillion in 2027. That's not a cut. Furchtgott-Roth points out that "the new budget also proposes to increase federal Medicaid spending from $378 billion a year today to $524 billion a year in 2027." That ain't a cut either. It's an increase.

She also notes that America has over 90 anti-poverty programs, 17 food aid programs and 22 housing assistance programs. You think this has been a success? I don't.

Adding up each and every new year between now and 2027, the federal government will spend about $55 trillion. Do we think that's enough? And the Trump budget would curb that by about 7 percent, or roughly $4 trillion. That's all that's happening.

So Mick Mulvaney is right: This is a growth budget. Not because it destroys all federal assistance but because it will reinstitute reforms put in place by Democrat Bill Clinton that will restore incentives to work and remove incentives to not work.

When people re-enter the labor force, it promotes growth. Workfare is better than welfare. And President Trump also aims for a big-bang growth booster with a cut in business tax rates for large and small companies, along with immediate expensing and repatriation.

President is a mighty hard job. Even if he drains the swamp just a wee bit, President Trump will still shake up the establishment.

Three Easy Pieces: A Simple
Get-It-Done-Now Economic Plan

June 9, 2017

Now that former FBI Director James Comey's hearing is complete, it's time for everybody to roll up their sleeves and go back to work on returning the country to prosperity. The most populist policy would be to restore a long-lasting deeply rooted prosperity for every single American.

President Donald Trump cannot let a deluge of distractions disrupt his and the Republican Party's plans for meaningful health care and tax reform. The accusations of Russian collusion, the fallout from the Comey hearing, the left-wing media's daily barrage of anti-Trump propaganda — these are all distractions. And the administration and GOP Congress are in great jeopardy if they get caught up in it and take their eyes of the policy ball.

They must get some degree of health care and tax reform done — this year, and with tangible results in the next several months. If they don't get it done, they're going to get creamed in the 2018 midterms.

I see two grounds for this prediction.

First, without results on health care and taxes, Trump and the GOP will not have taken steps to palpably improve the economy in terms of growth, jobs and wages.

Second, without results on health care and taxes, Trump and the GOP will have revealed that they can't govern. They were elected to govern, and they should be able to govern. Trump ran on growth, jobs and wages. He needs to deliver on growth, jobs and wages.

Earlier this week, economist Stephen Moore and I met with senior people in the West Wing — senior, senior, senior people. And we presented a simple get-it-done-now economic plan. We call it "three easy pieces" (like the old Jack Nicholson film "Five Easy Pieces"), which are the following: Lower the corporate tax rate from 35 percent to 15 percent. Grant immediate expensing for new business investment. And establish a one-time 10 percent rate for the repatriation of offshore cash.

It's a simple tonic that will restore capital formation, productivity, real wages and economic growth. And, in terms of political expediency, it's practical. It's about getting done what you can get done.

To be sure, the business tax cut is the key piece of these three easy pieces. With a 35 percent corporate tax rate, America is uncompetitive among developed nations in this regard. But that's not what's most important here. When business taxes are reduced, 70 percent of the benefits go to the wage-earning middle class. That's what's most important.

And a business tax cut is practical. It's right-now practical. There is widespread agreement in Washington, D.C., about the need for a business tax cut. And legislators can legally and technically attach corporate-tax-rate reduction to the health care reform bill in reconciliation in 2017.

Reconciliation can be nearly anything you want it to be. This can get done.

House Freedom Caucus Chairman and North Carolina Rep. Mark Meadows is absolutely right that the August recess should be canceled until this big-bang grand slam reconciliation package is complete.

I'll be working this summer. I dare say that most readers of this article will be working this summer. So why shouldn't official Washington work all summer?

If drain the swamp means less vacations, so be it.

Now, I'm not saying Steve Moore and I sold our plan to our West Wing audience. They listened. They pondered. They took notes. And we hope it's in play. There are no commitments, but it's cooking.

And all of it can be attached to the reconciliation bill. Leave the larger issues of personal tax reform and a tax system overhaul for next year. Just get this done.

And block out the silliness.

Russiagate. Comeygate. Whatever-the-media-invents-today-gate. These only distract from the real reasons Donald Trump was put in office and congressional Republicans were given one more chance. American voters want the policy results that will deliver a return to economic prosperity.

A corporate tax cut, cash expensing and repatriation put us back on the prosperity path.

Three easy pieces. Get it done.

Steve Scalise, Nancy Pelosi
and a Return to Civility

June 17, 2017

Sometimes terrible tragedies can bring us together, and I'm hopeful that somehow a lasting good will come out of the ballfield shooting in Alexandria, Virginia. And maybe even a rebirth of civility, which has virtually disappeared from politics, and perhaps our culture as well.

Rep. Steve Scalise, who's currently fighting it out in a hospital in Washington, D.C., is an old friend of mine. I watched as he rose through the House ranks to become the majority whip. Like everyone else, I'm praying for his full recovery. He's a wonderful man.

And, like most everyone else, I was happy to hear President Donald Trump talking about unity in the wake of the shooting. He said, "We are strongest when we are unified and when we work together for the common good."

I can say the same for House Speaker Paul Ryan, who, true to form, spoke beautifully and passionately from the House floor, saying, "An attack on one of us is an attack on all of us. ... I ask each of you to join me to resolve to come together."

But I want to put a spotlight on one person who really surprised me with unexpected remarks. She got me thinking — praying — that maybe, just maybe, some lasting good will come out of this tragedy.

House Minority Leader Nancy Pelosi also spoke on the House floor in the hours after the shooting. She said her prayers were with Scalise, the Capitol Police and the others hit on that ballfield.

And she said much more. "You may not know this, my colleagues, but every time I pray, which is very frequently, and certainly every Sunday, I pray for all of you. All of you, together," she said. "In the earlier years, I used to pray for your happiness, for the fact that we would work together, heed the words of President Kennedy in the closing of his inaugural address, when he said ... 'God's work must truly be our own.'"

That's a central theme in my book "JFK and the Reagan Revolution: A Secret History of American Prosperity," which I wrote with Brian Domitrovic. Presidents Reagan and Kennedy were civil in public, as they sought to persuade their opponents, not smear them. And they both reached across the aisle to achieve their policy goals.

It's something we need to return to — desperately. And Pelosi spoke in that spirit.

"How do we view what God's will is for us?" she asked. "How do we come together to give confidence to the American people? As our founders intended, we would have our disagreements and we would debate them, and we would have confidence in our beliefs and humility to listen to others."

To listen to others.

For a long time, I have been talking about the need for a rebirth of civility. We cannot continue the meanness, the personal slurs and the polarizing attacks, all of which are doing great harm to America.

And now, sparked by tragedy, Pelosi seems to have said: Let us come together. Let us have civility in our discussions. Let us have a sense of humanity, and maybe even a sense of caring. Let us pray for ourselves and the rest of the country. Let's do this together.

She did add: "And I pray for Donald Trump, that his presidency will be successful, and that his family will be safe. Because it is about family."

When did you ever think you would hear her say that? It was a welcome surprise.

No, I'm not here to defend her politics. I'm a conservative. She's a liberal. I have my beliefs. She has her beliefs. The battle of ideas must go on.

But our tone, our style, our civility, our ability to listen — it seems to me that those have been missing for so many years.

The blame is on all sides. It's in the executive branch, the Senate, the House. Let's add the media and academia, as well. No one in this game is clean.

The political divide is large — across taxes, health care and a whole raft of tough agenda items. I get that.

I'm just saying, if Nancy Pelosi, who has been in Washington a good long while, is coming out and speaking of unity, civility and humility, it's worth giving it a listen.

Many of my friends disagree with this Pelosi kudos. Some believe I am hopelessly naive. They may be right.

But right now, today, I choose to believe that she means for all of us to be calm, to be humble, to be civil and to work together.

I'm praying for that because, if that's the case, we will get important things done to help this country and one another.

Let's hope and pray that something is changing here.

Keeping Freedom and Growth in the Fourth

July 5, 2017

What is the Fourth of July? It's a wonderful time. We're outdoors. We're with family and friends. We're playing golf or fishing. There are barbecues and baseball games and fireworks and all that good stuff.

And beneath it all, supporting it all, there is freedom. Freedom. The Fourth of July is about freedom, if nothing else. America's freedom, of course. But a freedom that extends to all people. One that leads to greatness and prosperity. A freedom that has become the backbone of the world.

I would like to take a moment this holiday to revisit the sources of that freedom. They were outlined so eloquently in perhaps the greatest document ever written, the Declaration of Independence. And they're as crucial now as they were 241 years ago.

It's a well-known story. Back in 1776, the Continental Congress sought freedom from tyranny. Members said: "We're revolting against a British monarchy and parliament that doesn't represent us. We're rebelling against laws we don't control and are capricious to say the least."

To formalize this revolt, the congress formed a committee of five. Chosen were Thomas Jefferson, Robert Livingston, John Adams, Ben Franklin and Roger Sherman — a pretty spiffy group of thinkers and writers.

Their task was to draft a statement of independence — although what they came up with was so much more.

Their document, "The Unanimous Declaration of the Thirteen United States of America," was adopted on July 4, 1776, after days of debate and revision. The document begins: "When in the Course of human events, it becomes necessary for one people to dissolve the political bands which have connected them with another, and to assume among the powers of the earth, the separate and equal station to which the Laws of Nature and of Nature's God entitle them, a decent respect to the opinions of mankind requires that they should declare the causes which impel them to the separation."

I'd like to underscore the civility of that opening. This document is an example of civility. The great American revolt was a defense of the right of discussion. Civil discourse. Respectful disagreement.

Then there are "the Laws of Nature and of Nature's God." We derive our freedoms not from governments but from God. It was a revolutionary thought at a time when dictatorial monarchs across Europe believed they were gods.

Then we have perhaps the most famous sentence in the English language, if any language: "We hold these truths to be self-evident, that all men are created equal, that they are endowed by their Creator with certain unalienable Rights, that among these are Life, Liberty and the pursuit of Happiness."

That truly was revolutionary stuff. And it was beyond just the colonies.

The authors were saying, "We're speaking about the people here and oppressed peoples everywhere, those burdened with dictatorial who-cares-about-the-little-people governments.

And they spoke of life, liberty and the pursuit of happiness.

Life. Our very existence.

Liberty. You can't take my freedom away.

The pursuit of happiness. To live the way we want to live, to do the work we want to do, to marry who we want to marry, to have kids, accumulate property and be prosperous.

I've said this often: The most populist desire of the people of the United States and other free nations is long-lasting, deep-seated prosperity. Speaking of which, the long list of complaints against King George III's Britain included "cutting off our Trade with all parts of the world" (protectionism), "imposing Taxes on us without our Consent" (remedied with supply-side tax cuts) and (hat tip Seth

Lipsky of The New York Sun) a hint of stable money: "the amount and payment of" the judges' salaries.

But the Declaration critically goes on. It says: "That to secure these rights, Governments are instituted among Men, deriving their just powers from the consent of the governed, — That whenever any Form of Government becomes destructive of these ends, it is the Right of the People to alter or to abolish it, and to institute new Government."

Taking these statements together, we see a pecking order. There is God, a higher power or Nature's God, who grants us the unalienable rights of life, liberty and the pursuit of happiness. And whatever government is formed around this works for the people. And if the government lacks the consent of the people, there must be great change.

From the Lord to us, and then to government.

And when government breaks down, does poorly or becomes corrupt, it needs to be replaced one way or another.

There's a little bit of that going on today, is there not?

It's the Fourth of July. It's freedom day. The government works for us, not the other way around.

If it doesn't, the government gets kicked out on its keister.

Trump Has Putin Over a Barrel

July 8, 2017

A few years back, in one of his finest moments, Sen. John McCain said on a Sunday talk show, "Russia is a gas station masquerading as a country." It was right when he said it, and it's even more right today.

Russian President Vladimir Putin's circle of corrupt oligarchs gouge whatever money they can from the impoverished Russian economy and move it to bank accounts overseas. And they do this after giving Putin his cut, which he apparently also sends overseas.

Many say Putin is the richest man in Russia, worth billions and billions. So the old Soviet model of nomenklatura communist bureaucrats getting rich while the rest of the country declines is still in place.

But with energy prices falling, Putin's Russia has essentially been in a recession over the past four years. With oil at $50 a barrel or less, Russian budgets plunge deeper into debt. It's even doubtful the Russians have enough money to upgrade their military-energy industrial complex.

Through crafty media relations and his own bravado, a deluded Putin struggles to maintain the illusion that Russia is a strong economic power. But it ain't so. Not even close.

Now, Russia still has a lot of oil and gas reserves. And it uses this to bully Eastern and Western Europe. It threatens to cut off these resources if Europe dares to complain about Putin power grabs in Crimea, eastern Ukraine, the Baltics and elsewhere.

But enter President Donald Trump. In his brilliant speech in Warsaw, Poland, earlier this week, he called Putin's energy bluff.

It may well have been the best speech of his young presidency. Trump delivered a stirring leadership message, emphasizing the importance of God, freedom, strong families and democratic values.

And while unambiguously pledging to uphold NATO's Article 5 — which commits the members to protect one another — Trump went even deeper. "The fundamental question of our time is whether the West has the will to survive," he said. "Do we have the confidence in our values to defend them at any cost? ... if we do not have strong families and strong values, then we will be weak and we will not survive." He also spoke several times of the religious leadership and bravery of Pope John Paul II.

It was a bold strike for the West.

But in an absolutely *key* part of the speech, he took direct aim at Putin's energy bullying.

Trump said, "we are committed to securing your access to alternate sources of energy, so Poland and its neighbors are never again held hostage to a single supplier of energy."

President Trump has quickly made it clear that former President Barack Obama's war on business is over. He's also made it clear, through regulatory rollbacks of breathtaking scope, that the Obama war on fossil fuels is over.

Trump wants America to achieve energy dominance. He withdrew from the costly Paris climate accord, which would have severely damaged the American economy. He directed the EPA to rescind the Obama Clean Power Plan, which would have led to skyrocketing electricity rates. He fast-tracked the Keystone XL pipeline. He reopened the door for a modernized American coal industry. He's overturning all the Obama obstacles to hydraulic fracturing, which his presidential opponent Hillary Clinton would have dramatically increased. And he has opened the floodgates wide to energy exports.

Right now, U.S. oil reserves are almost in parity with those of Saudi Arabia. We have the second most coal reserves in the world. There are enough U.S. gas reserves to last us about a century. We have already passed Russia as the world's top natural gas producer. We are the world's top producer of oil and petroleum hydrocarbons. And exports of liquefied national gas are surging, with the

Department of Energy rapidly approving new LNG projects and other export terminals.

All these America-first energy policies are huge economic-growth and high-wage job producers at home. But in the Warsaw speech, Trump made it clear that America's energy dominance will be used to help our friends across Europe. No longer will our allies have to rely on Russia's Gazprom supplies with inflated, prosperity-killing prices.

In short, with the free market policies he's putting in place in America's energy sector and throughout the U.S. economy, the business man president fully intends to destroy Russia's energy-market share. And as that takes hold, Russia's gas station economy will sink further.

And as *that* takes hold, Bully-boy Putin will have to think twice about Ukraine, Poland and the Baltics. He'll have to think twice about his anti-American policies in the Middle East and North Korea. And he'll have to think twice about his increasingly precarious position as the modern-day Russian tsar.

And the world may yet become a safer place.

Trump has Putin over a barrel.

Big Economic Ideas From
Art Laffer and Steve Forbes

July 22, 2017

I participated in perhaps a bit of radio history last week when Steve Forbes and Art Laffer joined me on my syndicated radio show. It may have been the first time these supply-side economics giants were ever together over the airwaves.

Forbes, of course, is chairman of Forbes Media, and he twice ran brilliant issue campaigns for president. And Laffer, once a key adviser to President Ronald Reagan, is father to the groundbreaking Laffer Curve, for which he should have won a Nobel prize. In our discussion, they didn't disappoint. (For a full transcript, visit http://c10.nrostatic.com/sites/default/files/kudlow-transcript_20170715.html.)

We started with "one big idea." That's how the late Jack Kemp approached economic policy reform back in the 1980s. And his big idea, embraced by Reagan, was a mix of low marginal tax rates to spur economic growth incentives and a sound, reliable dollar to conquer inflation and create confidence. (This duplicated President John F. Kennedy's prosperity model, which Brian Domitrovic and I wrote about in "JFK and the Reagan Revolution.")

But these days, if you adhere to that big idea, you're ridiculed as clinging to the past. My guests would have none of it.

"We need it now more than ever," said Forbes. "To say that just because it worked 40 years ago, therefore it's old, is like saying the Declaration of Independence and the Constitution are old, therefore we can cast them aside."

Forbes' version of "one big idea" is a flat tax and a sound dollar linked to gold. If we have that, we'll be the "land of opportunity again."

Laffer agreed. "Our economic verities have remained forever," he said. "They go back to caveman, pre-cavemen. Incentives matter: If you reward an activity, then people do more of it. If you punish an activity, people do less of it."

But for the tax side of "one big idea," Laffer would like to see corporate-tax reform. I agree. Reagan used to say, "Give me half a loaf now, and I'll get the other half later." Well, I'd take the half-loaf of corporate tax cuts right now.

And that would work for Forbes, who can see income-tax reform following corporate-tax reform. Of President Trump, he said, "Even if we get to this two years down the road, I think he'd be amenable to doing something radical like a flat tax."

But why is it that our Democratic friends in the economics profession and politics work so hard to discredit the idea of lowering marginal tax rates on the extra dollar earned to spark the positive incentives that lead to prosperity?

"Let me put it just succinctly," answered Laffer. "These people are willing to rebut arguments they know to be true in order to curry favors with their political benefactors."

To which Forbes added: "A lot of these far-left ideologues would rather have a smaller economy and more government power than a bigger economy and a smaller government."

From that sad truth, we moved to prosperity killers — trade protectionism in particular, about which there is still much talk within the Trump camp. Where, I asked, does trade protectionism — including tariffs on China — fit into the low-tax-rate, strong-dollar prosperity model?

"It doesn't," said Forbes, who offered an alternative: "The smart approach is get this economy moving through these tax cuts and deregulation ... and then having a stable dollar, and then you sit down with country by country and remove trade barriers." Anything but the trade protectionism that blew up the stock market in 1929.

To which Laffer added the great line: "Don't just stand there; undo something!"

"Cut taxes, stabilize the dollar, reduce tariffs, reduce regulation," he said. "Undo, undo, undo and undo the damages these other guys have done."

One of those damages is Obamacare. And the fear now is that it will never get undone.

But my guests were optimistic, if philosophical. How will we get true free-market health care reform?

"You do this often, sometimes with great leaps but sometimes step by step," said Forbes, to which Laffer added: "With any type of change that we can make in the right direction ... never let the best be the enemy of the good."

Finally, I asked, "Is the free-market model losing ground?" We've seen its decline in Europe, Latin America and elsewhere.

"This thing always ebbs and flows," said Laffer. "Reagan, at first, was dissed by all the foreign leaders, except for Thatcher. And once our success story came in, he's now virtually a god. That's going to happen again, believe me."

The limits of this space have forced me to drastically abbreviate what I do believe was a historic radio event. Two economic giants met and discussed the big ideas that will restore growth and prosperity. They offered the "how" and were confident that the "when" is near.

Index Capital Gains for Inflation, Mr. President

August 12, 2017

President Donald Trump's pledge to "Make America Great Again" requires nothing less than reigniting economic growth and prosperity. Wealth creation is essential. As Congress pivots to tax reform — which is crucial to the wealth creation — the president could take matters into his own hands by issuing an executive order to index capital gains for inflation.

President Trump's absolute best economic policy so far has been his relentless rampage against onerous, burdensome, costly, prosperity-killing business regulations. And the taxation of inflationary capital gains fits right in there. It is an unfair and misguided policy that punishes risk and success. The president should use his executive authority — as he so often has to drain the swamp — to remove this prosperity-killing practice.

Consider this: You invest $1,000, and after 10 years, you sell that investment for $1,200. But if inflation averaged 2.5 percent in that period, the $1,200 you receive will be worth less in real terms than the $1,000 you invested. And yet, under current law, you will pay a tax on your $200 capital gain.

The results of this policy can be perverse. "As has been well documented," writes Alan Auerbach, an economist at the University of California, Berkeley, "realized capital gains may be subject to tax rates that easily exceed 100 percent of real gains in the presence of inflation."

But it's the law. And eliminating it would not only be the fair thing to do for investors — it would spark a wave of prosperity.

Gary Robbins, a former economist for the Department of Treasury, estimates that indexing capital gains for inflation this year would create an additional 400,000 jobs, grow the U.S. capital stock by $1.1 trillion, and boost GDP by roughly $500 billion by 2025. That all translates to an additional $3,600 for the average household.

President Reagan ushered in two decades of prosperity with his tax and regulatory policies, including an audacious (and sorely needed) measure to index much of the federal tax code for inflation. That capital gains indexation was not included in that measure has bedeviled economists who consider it bad policy to levy a tax on inflationary gains.

Congress has repeatedly toyed with legislation to index capital gains. In fact, a measure containing a fix for the problem landed on then-President Clinton's desk in 1995, only to be vetoed.

If President Trump wants to hear firsthand why capital gains indexation is so important, he need only speak with his vice president. In 2006, then-Rep. Mike Pence introduced legislation with 88 co-sponsors to index capital gains for assets held for more than three years.

Capital gains taxes totaled $134 billion last year. According to Robbins, approximately one-fourth of that revenue was generated by taxing inflationary gains. That translates to a $34 billion tax on phantom income.

Opponents of capital gains indexation say the associated revenue loss would be too great. But inasmuch as inflationary gains should not have been taxed in the first place, a revenue loss is a good thing. It represents the correction of a tax injustice.

But the second-order effects that Robbins documents should remove any reservations based on revenue loss. Without the federal tax on inflationary gains, asset prices will adjust until they reach a new, higher equilibrium. Shareholders and other investors will see their portfolios grow. And the federal government will collect billions of dollars in new tax revenue as taxpayers realize real capital gains.

Meanwhile, more investing and risk-taking will increase much-needed productivity, real worker wages and overall economic growth. Will real revenues rise as well? We betcha.

There is the question of whether the president has the legal authority to issue an executive order instructing the treasury secretary to issue new regulations to index the capital gains cost basis for inflation. The matter comes down to whether the governing Internal Revenue Code section covering the definition of the word "cost" is sufficiently ambiguous to allow regulatory reinterpretation. Congress never specifically mandated that "cost" was to be determined in nominal terms, nor did it prohibit the use of real valuation.

When President George H.W. Bush's administration looked into this 25 years ago, attorneys at the Justice Department and the Treasury Department concluded that the president lacked legal authority. However, according to a landmark paper by Charles Cooper and Vincent Colatriano that appeared several years ago in the Harvard Journal of Law & Public Policy, "jurisprudential developments over the last two decades have confirmed ... that Treasury has regulatory authority to index capital gains for inflation."

Former Federal Reserve Board Governor Wayne Angell correctly identifies the tax on phantom capital gains as "the worst aspect of the most damaging tax on capital." President Trump could solve this problem with the stroke of his pen and, in the process, promote economic growth and prosperity.

Trump Turnaround Puts New Tax-Cut Writing on the Wall

September 16, 2017

Financial markets and most media pundits are missing the new writing on the wall. For a variety of reasons surrounding shrewd moves by President Trump, the chances for significant tax cuts in the next 10 weeks have risen sharply.

Since the Charlottesville blowup in mid August, when the president's fortunes were at low ebb — and I'll repeat my view that there's not a racist, hateful, white supremacist bone in Trump's body — we've witnessed a dramatic executive turnaround. Trump beautifully handled the Harvey and Irma emergencies. His bipartisan political pivot to Senate Minority Leader Chuck Schumer and House Minority Leader Nancy Pelosi to keep the government open and raise the debt ceiling was clever indeed. As economist Steve Moore puts it, POTUS publicly spanked Republican leaders House Speaker Paul Ryan and Senate Majority Leader Mitch McConnell. And though there's plenty of confusion about immigration reform, it's clear now that 800,000 recipients of the Deferred Action for Childhood Arrivals program won't be deported for at least two years, if ever.

Some polls show the president's approval nearing 50 percent. The public likes what it sees.

And, most importantly, Trump has cleared the decks for tax cuts and reform.

Make no mistake: Trump is absolutely committed to tax cuts. This is completely unlike the health care muddle. And critical here is the argument Trump is making: A big drop in large- and small-business tax rates will mostly benefit middle-class wage earners.

Research from Kevin Hassett, formerly of the American Enterprise Institute, or AEI, and now chairman of the White House Council of Economic Advisers, shows that about 70 percent of the benefits of business tax cuts going to wage earners. This is not a tax cut for the rich, as Johnny-One-Note Democrats insist.

There are two big numbers standing atop Trump's tax plan: 3 percent and 15 percent. Three percent is the new growth path that will normalize America's economy and generate at least $3 trillion of additional revenues over 10 years (or sooner). This is the mother of all pay-fors. Fifteen percent is the corporate rate that will spur increases in capital formation, business investment, productivity and real wages.

The Republican establishment says it can't be done. It'll only risk dropping the business rate from 35 to 25 percent. But Trump wants the full 15. So does his Treasury secretary, Steven Mnuchin. Other than the president, Mnuchin, whom I call the "apostle of growth," is the only administration official to keep up the drumbeat for 3 and 15 percent.

Aparna Mathur of AEI notes that at 39.1 percent, including state taxes, the U.S. has the highest statutory rate among G-20 nations. (China is 15 percent.) And our average corporate rate, which is total taxes paid as a share of income, is 29 percent, third highest in the G-20.

So, echoing the president, if we want to build out investment, jobs and wages, bring back overseas profits, stop American companies from going overseas and make the investment climate in America top in the world, we need a big-bang slash of our business tax rate.

It's not a matter of bean counting. It's a matter of growth-oriented economic policy.

Trump is ending former President Obama's wars on business and success. He's halting the war on fossil fuels. And he's virtually rolling back the regulatory state. The Office of Management and Budget reports that roughly 800 pending regulations have been frozen, rolled back or reclassified in the administration's first seven months.

Slashing the business tax rate is the necessary complement to this regulatory relief.

And GOP lawmakers have 10 weeks to do it.

Can they? Will they?

Here's some progress: It looks like House Speaker Paul Ryan is taking off his Congressional Budget Office green eyeshades. Rather than insist on "revenue-neutral" tax policy, he seems to be returning to his Jack Kemp supply-side roots, arguing that growth is the most important issue.

The CBO is a big part of the swamp that President Trump would drain. With its pathetically small growth estimates, it blocks pro-growth tax-cut policies. Neither the CBO nor the Joint Committee on Taxation has any serious models showing how lower tax rates reduce tax avoidance and tax sheltering — a point made emphatically by supply-side mentor Arthur Laffer.

But Mnuchin's Treasury will come up with more realistic models for the Trump tax cut. And there's no reason why these estimates couldn't be used.

What's more, there's no reason why the 10-year scorecard window can't be extended to 20 years. The green-eyeshade process must not be permitted to block an American prosperity renaissance.

The GOP needs a budget resolution, which will contain crucial 51-vote reconciliation instructions on spending and taxes. But where there's strong political will, legislative ways and means will be found. Ten weeks is plenty of time.

So I agree with my friends at Bretton Woods Research: Budget and tax-cut draft legislation is coming sooner than folks think. My financial take? Buy stocks, go long the dollar and short gold.

In other words, optimism.

Trump's Incentive-Packed Tax Plan

October 2, 2017

Much as he did in his command performance before the United Nations, when he took back control of U.S. foreign policy, President Donald Trump has seized and energized the tax cut issue. Almost daily, he is pounding away on the themes of faster economic growth and more take-home pay, arguing that his plan will make America's economy great again.

This is Trumpian leadership at its best.

"Under my administration," Trump just told the National Association of Manufacturers, "the era of economic surrender is over."

The Trump plan would slash large- and small-business tax rates, double the standard deduction for middle-income folks, make the whole tax code simpler by eliminating unnecessary deductions, repeal the death tax and end the alternative minimum tax.

As usual, Democrats say the president's plan is a handout to the rich. But in a recent speech in Indianapolis, Trump asked: Why can't this be a bipartisan tax cut bill? He even quoted Democrat John F. Kennedy, who said, "The right kind of tax cut at the right time ... is the most effective measure that this government could take to spur our economy forward."

He also reminded his audience that President Reagan's tax cuts were passed with significant bipartisan majorities.

But today's Democrats have written JFK's tax story out of the history books (never mind Reagan's).

Key tax-writing committees are now polishing the Trump plan, fine-tuning it to pass the Senate with 51 votes. But there are a couple of key points that need clarifying.

The argument that the U.S. is doomed to 2 percent or less growth — "secular stagnation" no matter what we do in terms of tax policy — is nonsense. Across-the-board tax cuts produced 5 percent annual growth during the JFK period. And after tax cuts were fully implemented in 1983, real growth averaged 4.6 percent for the remainder of Reagan's presidency.

Treasury Secretary Steven Mnuchin and National Economic Council Director Gary Cohn are touting the 3 percent growth scenario, saying it will pay for the tax cuts. But the naysayers refuse to admit that tax rate incentives matter.

OK, let's take one example from the Trump tax plan. Corporations today are taxed at 35 percent. That means, for every extra dollar of profit, a company keeps 65 cents. But the president has agreed on a 20 percent corporate tax rate. So, for the extra dollar earned, the private company would keep 80 cents.

That's a *massive* 23 percent incentive reward. Do we really think businesses will not be affected by this? That defies logic.

And as supply-side mentor Art Laffer points out, the incentive reward of a lower business tax rate will reduce tax avoidance and sheltering. It's another solid point mainstream economists continue to ignore.

But the incentive effects don't stop there. The key to wage growth is productivity. Think of it as efficiency. And large and small businesses need new capital investment to modernize equipment and better train an efficient workforce.

Yet real wages have barely increased since 2000, alongside virtually no productivity increases and a huge slump in capital formation. That's the missing link between a 2 and a 3 percent economy.

Rather than punish investment, the Trump plan will spur growth across the board. Everyone will benefit.

The supply-side incentive effect also includes the repatriation of trillions of U.S. company dollars lodged overseas to avoid taxes, as well as 100 percent expensing write-offs for new investment of any kind.

Taken together, this plan contains a mountain of incentives.

On the individual side, the sleeper tax detail is the doubling of the standard deduction. As my CNBC colleague Jake Novak points out, this is a huge positive for young millennials (who don't own much) and folks with no mortgages or homes. It puts more cash in worker's pockets, simplifies the code and means that near 80 percent of taxpayers won't have any deductions.

Slimming income-tax rates from seven to three brackets and cutting income-tax rates in general add even more supply-side incentives to the Trump package.

More money for rich people? Well, the not-rich family of four will be a lot better off with a $24,000 standard deduction. And the center-right Tax Foundation calculates that the bottom 80 percent of households get a lower tax burden, while the top 20 percent get a higher burden.

The Republican Party has got to win this issue, preferably this year.

So, a warning: The GOP cannot let archaic process rules prevent good policy. Rules can be changed. CBO estimates can be ignored. Parliamentarian decisions can be overridden.

Play hardball, GOP. JFK did it. Reagan did it. And now you have Donald Trump doing it — using all his energy to get a big tax cut that will return prosperity to America's workers and families and enhance our strength overseas.

Kevin Hassett Spanks the
Tax Policy Center

October 9, 2017

President Trump's new chair of the Council of Economic Advisers, Kevin Hassett, walked into the lion's den last week with his first official speech. He used the moment to pound the leftist Tax Policy Center. It was a wonderful sight.

When Hassett wasn't pounding the TPC, he was spanking them. He took them to the woodshed, and disciplined them in public view.

Hassett rightfully accused the TPC for ignoring widely accepted economic literature, for using false assumptions on tax details that have never been published, and for manufacturing income-redistribution ("tax cuts for the rich") and deficit numbers that don't even exist.

"It's inaccurate," he said. "It's fiction."

In perhaps his toughest criticism of all, Hassett called the TPC's findings "scientifically indefensible." There's no greater insult among academics.

It's a pity that mainstream media outlets refer to the TPC as "nonpartisan." They're not. TPC staff is chock-full of former Obama economists.

But Hassett has shown no fear.

Kevin Hassett is the new face at the highest economic level of the Trump administration. But he's no neophyte. He has a Ph.D. in economics from the University of Pennsylvania. He has spent time on the staff of the Federal Reserve Board in Washington. He taught at Columbia Business School. He was a long-time economic-policy director at AEI.

And he's well-liked by everyone who knows him. Plus, he's smart. Very smart.

Not only did he chastise the TPC, he schooled them on a number of important tax policies that have become mainstream thinking inside the Trump White House.

Sighting numerous peer-reviewed papers, Hassett reminded his audience of a plain truth: Taxes matter. They impact the economy.

"Economists who have studied the effects of taxes over time have discovered a consensus," he said. "Lower marginal tax rates and a broader base increase the rate of economic growth and well-being." (Italics mine.)

He continues: "For years, TPC analyzed tax bills without providing dynamic scoring, but now provides a dynamic score, but with zero effect."

For me, Hassett's biggest contribution to the tax debate is the notion that high corporate tax rates depress the wages of workers.

Because companies have stashed profits overseas, and because the U.S. tax cost of investment is so high, middle-income wage earners have suffered mightily. Hassett — and his AEI colleague Aparna Mathur — have argued for over a decade that if you want to raise wages, cut corporate tax rates.

During his TPC speech, Hassett noted that "for the median household in the U.S., the top corporate marginal rate cut from 35 percent to 20 percent would boost wage growth almost four-fold."

In his past work, Hassett has argued that 70 percent of the benefits of lower business tax rates accrue to middle-income wage earners — in other words, Donald Trump's middle-class base.

Trump's tax cuts are not handouts to the rich, as the redistributionist Democratic left argues. Everyone benefits from these lower tax rates. As JFK put it, a rising tide lifts all boats. The growth ignited by lower tax rates solves all problems.

Class warfare has never worked in American politics. But Trump's tax plan will help middle-income wage earners the most. There's nothing wrong with that.

Backing up Hassett's assertions, former CEA chair Glenn Hubbard recently wrote in the Wall Street Journal that too many economists fail to consider the share of the U.S. corporate tax burden borne by labor — 60 percent according to his research. Neither the TPC, the Congressional Budget Office, nor the Joint Tax Committee model these results. Instead, they ignore the evidence.

A recent analysis of the House tax plan — which is nearly identical to the Trump plan — by professors Alan Auerbach (University of California, Berkeley) and Laurence Kotlikoff (Boston University) concluded that it would boost wages by 8 percent. That's a big number.

It's the difference between a prospering and optimistic middle class and a pessimistic middle class that lives day to day, paycheck to paycheck.

I look at it this way: Trump's tax-cut and regulatory-rollback policies are aimed directly at ending the war on business, which has dragged down the economy for nearly two decades. Let's *reward* success rather than punish it.

In just eight months, this growth message has generated a whopping increase in business and consumer confidence. The economy is picking up steam. The stock market has been on a tear. This is not a coincidence.

If Trump continues to link large- and small-business tax cuts to the well-being of the wage-earning middle class, he'll score economic victories across the board. At the same time, America will regain the populist prosperity that's been the backbone of our democracy for nearly 250 years.

That's right. As I sometimes put it, free-market capitalism is the best path to prosperity.

It's comforting to know Kevin Hassett is burning this torch down in the swamp of Washington, D.C.

President Trump Needs a Stable Dollar Along With Tax Cuts to Maximize Growth

October 28, 2017

President Trump is likely to name a new Federal Reserve chair over the next few days. Speculation is focused on current Fed governor Jay Powell and Stanford University economist John Taylor. The list may be larger; it could still include current Chair Janet Yellen or Kevin Warsh. Trump is soliciting opinions and advice from people inside and outside government. We will see soon enough.

Unfortunately, so much of the conversation about a new Fed leader is focused on who will be the high-interest-rate hawk or the low-interest-rate dove. But that's not really the way we should be looking at it.

Here's a point no one has discussed: the fate of the dollar.

Now, strictly speaking, dollar policy is the purview of the Treasury Department, which has the authority to intervene in exchange markets to buy or sell dollars. By the way, Congress also has a constitutional prerogative to set dollar value.

During the 1990s, Democrat Robert Rubin was secretary of the Treasury, and he advocated a strong-dollar policy. Just in case markets didn't believe him, he intervened a couple of times, buying dollars to punctuate his policy.

But the Fed and its money-creating balance-sheet policies must work with the Treasury to execute dollar policies. In the long run, Treasury interventions don't really have any clout. It's the Fed that really counts.

And yet, we don't really know what dollar policies the Fed candidates favor.

So far as I know, Yellen hardly ever mentions the dollar. Nor does Powell, at least not in his very few public speeches.

While President Trump sometimes publicly favors a steady dollar, he sometimes warns that he does not want a particularly strong greenback.

But I think the best policy is a steady, sound, reliable King Dollar.

If you look at periods of dollar weakness, especially the 1970s but also the 2000s, a sinking dollar is usually associated with rising inflation, higher interest rates and damage to the economy. In these circumstances, investors at home and abroad lose confidence and take their money elsewhere.

President George W. Bush's pro-growth tax cuts were partly nullified by a sinking dollar. Yet when Presidents John F. Kennedy and Ronald Reagan slashed marginal tax rates, they also favored a sound dollar. (I covered this at length with Brian Domitrovic in our book, "JFK and the Reagan Revolution.") Low taxes and a stable dollar was a winning combination that promoted economic growth without inflation.

There's a lesson to be learned here. But we haven't really seen the Fed reference the dollar for many years. It seems not to be part of its flawed and outdated economic models.

By the way, it's not just the dollar's exchange rate with other currencies; the value of our money should also be judged by forward-looking, inflation-sensitive market indicators, such as commodities, gold and Treasury bond spreads.

Warsh has warned that the central bank should not rely on labor-market indicators to gauge future inflation. He instead advocates a market-based price rule. This is similar to the approach used by Reagan Fed appointees Wayne Angell, Robert Heller, Manley Johnson and, for most of his term, Alan Greenspan.

And Taylor is working on a study that argues for a return to a rules-based international currency system. Several years ago, former Fed Chair Paul Volcker, who used gold and commodities as leading inflation indicators while appointed, argued for a rules-based monetary policy at home and new international currency cooperation abroad.

So if President Trump gets his tax cuts and continues his regulatory rollbacks, the economy will return to its historic norm of 3 to 4 percent growth. And faster real growth will lead to higher real interest rates and a higher real-exchange-rate value for our money.

As business anticipates much-needed tax cuts, the dollar is rising; gold is falling; and growth moves to 3 percent with minimal inflation.

This is a good thing. We're not talking about a skyrocketing currency and interest rates but important adjustments to pro-growth economic policies.

But we won't get there without a stable dollar.

If the White House, the Treasury and the Fed try to intervene for a weaker dollar, they will soon run into trouble. The tax cuts could be neutralized. Long, dormant inflation may reappear. And interest rates will wind up going much higher than otherwise would be the case.

It's a shame no one has directly asked the Fed candidates about the dollar, because more people working successfully for higher wages in a strong-growth economy do not cause inflation, as Fed models unfortunately predict. But a sinking greenback will.

A Pro-Growth Tax Bill Is on the Way

November 11, 2017

As the House and Senate work their way through the tax cut and reform effort, let me make one thing clear: Both plans are pro-growth, with the economic power coming from the business side. And where it comes from the personal side, there will be very little growth. That was always been the bet.

During the spring and summer of 2016, economist Steve Moore and I, working with Trump campaign officials Steven Mnuchin and Stephen Miller, saw major tax reductions for large and small businesses as the centerpiece of the candidate's tax policy. Whatever Congress came up with on the personal side, so be it.

So, one way or another — even with the glitches and differences between the House and Senate tax plans — Congress will come up with a significant pro-growth bill because business tax cuts are still the centerpiece. And they should do it this year.

I spoke at a Senate Republican breakfast in Washington, D.C., last Tuesday. The whole leadership was there. And I observed a total commitment among the GOP senators to get a tax bill through by year-end. This will not be another health care breakdown.

Particularly after recent GOP electoral setbacks, the party knows it needs a strong tax-cut and economic-growth narrative for the 2018 midterms. If Republicans don't get it, they'll lose control of Congress. And if they do get it, they may pick up seats.

The political stakes are high.

As mentioned, there are glitches in both the Senate and House tax plans. But most of them can be corrected. And the differences between the two plans should narrow in conference.

The all-important business tax rate will come down to 20 percent from 35 percent. That's the key to economic growth. And the biggest beneficiaries will be middle-class wage earners.

The issue of small-business pass-throughs is not completely resolved. It seems the Senate has a better take on this than the House. But there's a small-business tax cut coming.

The Senate's idea to phase in the new corporate tax rate in 2019 is a bad idea. (President Trump agrees.) To be sure, the GOP senators want full cash expensing for capex projects for 2018. Good. But as economist Art Laffer warns, if you hold back the actual rate reduction, you'll see a lot of tax avoidance and sheltering next year.

That will include offshoring. A delay will deter foreign companies from coming to the United States. You may wind up losing revenues — perhaps $100 billion.

On the House side, the so-called bubble rate of 45.6 percent is also not a good idea. It's being done to claw back the 12 percent rate high-end earners move through on the way to 40 percent. But why punish success?

Those upper-end folks are largely investment-oriented. As FedEx CEO Fred Smith says, it's time to stop punishing investment. That includes businesses and individuals.

Let the Democrats be the class warriors who tax the rich. The GOP stands for growth.

I assume this will be fixed in conference.

There are other issues. The personal side is a mishmash of credits and deductions. This is no Ronald Reagan bill of 1986. Good tax reform slashes individual rates so that reductions and loopholes are no longer necessary.

But there's no slashing on the personal side, and it will be a fight over deductions. And, frankly, I'm underwhelmed by the deduction part.

I keep thinking: Why didn't the House and Senate simply agree on a 3 percent growth rate? And why haven't they embraced the Trump administration's argument that the business tax cuts will pay for themselves and generate 3 percent growth over the next decade?

House and Senate negotiators agreed on a 2.6 percent growth baseline. It's better than the Congressional Budget Office's 1.9

percent. But with 3 percent, they would have picked up $500 to $700 billion in additional revenues from faster growth.

Unfortunately, no model captures the significant pro-growth effects of international flows, such as repatriation and the possible capital inflow from foreign companies. Is it possible this could be changed in conference? Just a thought.

Of course, the old Byrd rule bugaboo is back. It annuls tax cuts if they promote deficits after 10 years.

So here's another thought: Senate Majority Leader Mitch McConnell used the nuclear option to end the filibuster on Supreme Court justice Neil Gorsuch. Why not nuclear-option the Byrd rule? Vice President Mike Pence is ready in the wings to override any objection.

The GOP must not let process stop growth-producing tax cuts. Growth is too important.

So let's play hardball, GOP, and do what's necessary to get these pro-growth tax cuts legislated and signed before year-end.

That will move the American economy back to the top of the worldwide heap. As Presidents John F. Kennedy and Ronald Reagan argued, when we are strong at home, we're strong abroad.

I'd Vote for It. You Should, Too

November 5, 2017

Warts and all, if I were a voting member of Congress, I would certainly cast a yea for the tax-cut plans passed by the Senate and House that are headed for conference (to work out minor differences) in the weeks ahead.

These bills are not perfect, especially on the individual side. But the business tax cuts will generate an investment boom in the years ahead. And those cuts will bring economic growth back to its historical norm of 3 to 4 percent.

Incredibly, the Joint Committee on Taxation, or JTC, scored growth for the Senate plan at less than 1 percent. So much for its "dynamic" model. The Tax Foundation estimates 3 to 5 percent growth over the next 10 years. That's more like it, but it's still too low.

Look, the central cause of the 2-percent real-GDP growth slump over the past 17 years has been a lack of capital formation with virtually no real business investment, flattened productivity and barely any increase in real workforce wages.

Yet the tax plans under discussion — which go back to the work of economist Steve Moore, Treasury Secretary Steven Mnuchin, White House senior adviser Stephen Miller, economist Art Laffer, Forbes Media Chairman and Editor-in-Chief Steve Forbes and myself — are remarkably similar to the Trump campaign draft on the business side.

So I can say with confidence that the current tax package is directly aimed at reducing the current high tax cost of capital and increasing after-tax returns from investment.

Incentives matter. If it pays more after tax to build new capital stock and generate more business-equipment investment, people will do so. This is standard economics.

There may be disagreements on the numerical effects, but the principle has worked in the past (with Presidents Kennedy and Reagan) and will work in the future.

A 20-percent corporate tax rate, immediate full expensing, repatriation of U.S. corporate cash overseas and a 23-percent discount for subchapter S corporation pass-throughs (much credit to Sen. Ron Johnson for this) will generate way more growth and investment than mainstream forecasters suggest.

At various times, President Trump has talked about 3 percent, 4 percent and even 5 percent growth. Despite the dreary mainstream models, I believe the president will turn out to be correct.

What's more, faster economic growth will generate much higher tax revenues. From businesses to investors to entrepreneurial startups, less tax avoidance and sheltering will raise revenues far beyond the standard consensus estimate.

Supply-siders like myself always buck the trend on pricing out lower tax rates. But again, we were right in the '60s, '80s and '90s running against the tide. So I suggest history will repeat itself.

By the way, in terms of the revenue hunt going on in Congress, I wish somebody would look at the lowball estimates compiled by the JTC with respect to repatriation. It estimates $25 billion in 2018, $21 billion in 2019, and $6 billion to $7 billion in the three years following. This is nuts.

Assuming about $3 trillion coming back home at an average tax rate of 10 percent, that's $300 billion in new revenues — way beyond the JTC estimate. And that's conservative. It could be $350 billion in the first year or two, which would be substantially more revenue and a way bigger pay-for than what the JTC predicts.

And there's more on the dynamic side. Booming stock market gains of roughly $6 trillion as of late could generate another $600 or $700 billion in revenues from capital gains, as well as hundreds of billions of dollars more in dividends, which generate massive revenue increases.

None of this is scored. The government forecasters don't understand international flows and the interactions of stocks, capital gains and dividends. Their estimates are probably several trillion revenue dollars short.

Sure, there are things on the individual side that should be changed. Personal tax rates should be much lower. A backdoor capital-gains tax hike on individual investors must be erased. And the proliferation of tax credits is inefficient and complex with no marginal incentives to promote growth.

Yes, everybody likes kids. But not everyone has them. And a lot of people like dogs and cats. Shouldn't they get tax credits, too? No. If you're looking for more money in your pocket, more take-home pay, the best prescription is to slash personal tax rates for everyone.

(By the way, why didn't Congress end the carried-interest loophole for private-equity firms?)

But here's the crux of the matter: An investment boom generating much faster growth will benefit everyone. Small businesses, new businesses, investors and wage earners will all prosper from a tax-cut-led investment boom.

Yes, a rising tide will lift all boats. The great news is that President Trump, the Senate and the House are absolutely moving in the right direction — and gathering momentum on the way.

I'd vote for it. You should, too.

Republicans' Tax Plan Takes a Quirky Swipe at the Little Guys

By Lawrence Kudlow & Stephen Moore
December 12, 2017

Republicans are supposed to be the party that cuts the job-killing capital gains tax, not raises it. But because of a quirk in the Senate-passed tax bill, the tax on capital gains may go up — and for some types of long-held assets, fairly substantially.

Most members of Congress don't even know of this stealth capital gains hike. Here's the story: At the start of the year, Republicans promised to reverse the near-60 percent rise in the capital gains tax under former President Barack Obama — a hike that helped bring investment rates to historic lows. The GOP plan was to eliminate the Obamacare 3.8 percent investment-tax surcharge on capital gains and dividends?. That repeal never happened. But now, the Senate tax-reform bill proposes to raise several billion over the next decade by changing the rules on how stocks are taxed.

It would require shareholders to sell their oldest shares in a company before their newest purchased ones. The older the share, the larger the taxable capital gain. This is called the first-in, first-out accounting system.

Consider this example: Let's say you bought 100 shares of Apple stock in 1998 at $100 a share?, and then you bought another 100 shares in 2008 at $300 each. If you were to sell 100 shares at $500 a share, you would have to "sell" the oldest stock and pay a $400 per share capital gains tax, versus $200 a share under the current law.

Now, this accounting change may actually make sense, except that the gains on long-term stocks are not adjusted for inflation. So on many sales of long-held stock, as much as half of the reported and taxable "gain" is due to the compounding effect of inflation. The actual capital gains tax paid could more than double for many stock and asset sales.

Therefore, the Senate rules would require millions of Americans to pay taxes on phantom or illusory gains. That is patently unfair and would discourage the very long-term investment that economists and politicians agree that we need.

If you were to give us $1,000 today, we would be glad to give you $1,500 25 years from now, because inflation is likely to run ahead of that pace. Believe us — you haven't made a $500 profit on this transaction. But the government thinks you have.

There are other huge inequities in this new policy. Under the Senate bill, there's an exception for mutual funds, exchange-traded funds and other institutional funds. They would continue to apply the tax treatment under current law.

So get this: The little guy who wants to buy and sell stock on his own has to pay the higher capital gains tax, but the big investment funds have a more generous set of rules with lower taxes. Huh?

The mutual-fund industry convinced the Senate that conforming to the new rule would be too complicated. That's good news for Fidelity Investments and Vanguard. But what about Joe Lunchbucket? This new rule is complicated for him, too. This law is going to nearly force small investors to purchase stock through the big fund managers — and, of course, pay their fees.

Most important, this is bad for the economy. The higher tax penalty on investment would discourage people from buying stock or investing in small startup companies in the first place.

This would also exacerbate the lock-in effect of the capital gains tax. History shows that when the tax on gains is higher, Americans are much more reluctant to sell their shares and pay the higher tax. This benefits old, established companies like Boeing and Microsoft but dries up capital for smaller, fast-growing firms that could be the next-generation Apple, Google or Uber.

In other words, this stealth capital gains tax contradicts the entire purpose of an otherwise prosperity-generating tax bill. We want lower business tax rates and investment tax rates to get more growth, more jobs and higher wages. A backdoor capital gains tax would accomplish the opposite.

With This Tax Cut, Trump and the GOP Are on the Side of the Growth Angels

December 25, 2017

With President Trump's signing of the big tax cut bill, the Republican Party snatched victory from the jaws of defeat. Suddenly, the political and economic landscapes have changed. The GOP has turned the tables on the Democrats.

With the passage of this powerful tax-cut legislation to boost business investment, wages and take-home family pay, Trump and the GOP are on the side of the growth angels. The Democrats, meanwhile, are left with stale class-warfare slogans about tax cuts for the rich.

Ironically, government unions, with their pension plans heavily invested in equity shares, will benefit hugely from the tax-cut-led stock market boom. They boo the GOP bill while they should be cheering.

But there's a lot of irony to go around. Unlike the pro-growth tax-cut party of former President John F. Kennedy, today's left-lurching Democrats root against economic growth, the stock market and a powerful prosperity at home that lends strength abroad. This is not a good place for Democrats to be.

If the supply-side business tax cuts perform as well as I believe they will, Trump and the GOP, with the stroke of a pen, will have greatly enhanced their outlook for the midterm elections.

One of the more incredible things about this story is the almost immediate support of large companies. Bank of America announced a $1,000 bonus for about 145,000 employees in response to the tax-cut bill. And AT&T and Comcast announced $1,000 bonuses for more than 300,000 people combined, along with substantial new investments in the United States. Ditto investments for Boeing. And more banks have joined the parade. Wells Fargo, PNC, BB&T and Fifth Third Bancorp are raising their minimum wages to $15 an hour.

All this is tied to a massive corporate tax rate deduction from 35 to 21 percent. This is the most powerful growth measure in the plan. Trump called these workers' bonuses tax "love" in a tweet.

At the old 35 percent rate, our companies took home 65 cents on the extra dollar. At the new 21 percent rate, they'll take home 79 cents. This enormous 21 percent incentive rewards new risk-taking, investment, a recycling of overseas profits to the U.S. and additional after-tax profitability.

Combined with 100 percent immediate cash write-offs for new investment and the one-time repatriation of foreign-held earnings, this is the largest supply-side stimulus since 1986.

The result will be a business boom, where new capital formation and productivity increases the economy's potential to grow. This is counter-inflationary. We can say goodbye to 1 or 2 percent secular stagnation and hello to 3 to 4 percent long-run prosperity. And when you toss in lower marginal tax rates for individuals and the doubling of the standard deduction, you have even more potential for growth.

In a recent Tax Foundation analysis by President Scott Hodge, he notes that even the lowball Joint Committee on Taxation agrees the tax cuts pay for themselves. How? More gross domestic product will be generated than revenues lost to the Treasury. For every dollar lost, the tax cuts produce roughly $1.90 in additional GDP.

Also from the Tax Foundation is the assertion that the biggest tax liability reductions will come to the middle class, as shown through several examples. A single parent who earns $52,000 and has two children claims a 36 percent reduction in tax liabilities. A single-earner married couple with two children that makes $85,000 and files jointly gets a 20 percent tax-revenue reduction. And a married single-earner couple with two children that files jointly and earns $2 million only gets a 3 percent reduction in tax liabilities. So much for the tax-cuts-for-the-rich argument.

Let's not forget that the plan includes Arctic National Wildlife Refuge drilling access and the repeal of the Obamacare individual mandate. Let's also not forget the Trump administration's massive reductions of burdensome business regulations.

At the end of the day, the success of the Trump tax cuts will not be decided by Democrat-leaning polls or highly flawed econometric models. The proof in this pudding will be in the eating.

With the supply-side model of lower marginal tax-rate incentives to work, save and invest, plus significantly less tax avoidance and sheltering, the economy will move back to its normal steady-state pattern of 3 to 4 percent growth.

Already in the past two quarters we've seen a bump in business-equipment investment, producing better than 3 percent growth. The fourth quarter is likely to remain above 3 percent. The results of lower withholding rates accompanied by higher income-bracket thresholds will show up in February.

More take-home pay is always a winner. And businesses large and small are beginning to pull the investment trigger. Yes, the middle class will benefit. But everyone will profit from the first business boom in over 20 years.

President Kennedy, President Ronald Reagan, the late Jack Kemp, economist Art Laffer and the rest of the supply-side clan — which now includes Donald Trump — believes that a rising tide lifts all boats.

So which is better: 1 to 2 percent stagnation, or 3 to 4 percent prosperity?

Let the voters decide next year. But I'm taking the high ground.

About the Author

Lawrence Kudlow is CEO of Kudlow & Co. LLC, an economic and investment research firm in New York City.

Kudlow previously hosted CNBC's "The Kudlow Report" and "Kudlow & Company. He is also an economics commentator for CNBC. He hosts a weekly Saturday radio show on WABC Radio.

Kudlow is a nationally syndicated columnist, a contributing editor of National Review magazine, as well as a columnist and economics editor for National Review Online. He is the author of "American Abundance: The New Economic and Moral Prosperity," published by Forbes in January 1998.

Kudlow is consistently ranked one of the nation's premier and most accurate economic forecasters according to The Wall Street Journal semiannual forecasting survey.

He is a distinguished scholar of the Mercatus Center at George Mason University in Arlington, Virginia.

In 2005, New York Gov. George Pataki appointed Kudlow chairman of the New York State Tax Reform Commission.

For many years, Kudlow served as chief economist for a number of Wall Street firms. Kudlow was a member of the Bush-Cheney Transition Advisory Committee. During President Reagan's first term, Kudlow was the associate director for economics and planning for the Office of Management and Budget within the Executive Office of the President, where he was engaged in the development of the administration's economic and budget policy.

He is a trusted adviser to many of our nation's top decision-makers in Washington and has testified as an expert witness on economic matters before several congressional committees. He has also presented testimony at several Republican Governors Conferences.

Kudlow began his career as a staff economist at the Federal Reserve Bank of New York, working in the areas of domestic open-market operations and bank supervision.

Kudlow was educated at the University of Rochester and Princeton University's Woodrow Wilson School of Public and International Affairs. He is a member of The Union League Club, the Capitol Hill Club and the Women's National Republican Club. Kudlow is an avid tennis player and golfer. He and his wife, Judy, live in New York City and Redding, Connecticut.

INSANITY ONCE MORE
is also available as an e-book
for Kindle, Amazon Fire, iPad, Nook and
Android e-readers. Visit
creatorspublishing.com to learn more.

o o o

CREATORS PUBLISHING

We publish books.
We find compelling storytellers and
help them craft their narrative,
distributing their novels and collections
worldwide.

o o o

Made in United States
Troutdale, OR
01/22/2025

28190747R00106